Football Development Index

Football Development Index

Rationale, Methodology, and Application

Anatoly Vorobyev, Ilya Solntsev,
and Nikita Osokin

LEXINGTON BOOKS
Lanham • Boulder • New York • London

Published by Lexington Books
An imprint of The Rowman & Littlefield Publishing Group, Inc.
4501 Forbes Boulevard, Suite 200, Lanham, Maryland 20706
www.rowman.com

Unit A, Whitacre Mews, 26-34 Stannary Street, London SE11 4AB

Copyright © 2018 by Lexington Books

All rights reserved. No part of this book may be reproduced in any form or by any electronic or mechanical means, including information storage and retrieval systems, without written permission from the publisher, except by a reviewer who may quote passages in a review.

British Library Cataloguing in Publication Information Available

Library of Congress Cataloging-in-Publication Data

ISBN 978-1-4985-5519-7 (cloth : alk. paper)
ISBN 978-1-4985-5520-3 (electronic)

∞™ The paper used in this publication meets the minimum requirements of American National Standard for Information Sciences—Permanence of Paper for Printed Library Materials, ANSI/NISO Z39.48-1992.

Printed in the United States of America

Contents

Abbreviations — vii

Acknowledgments — ix

Introduction — xi

1. Conceptualization of Football Development — 1
2. Overview of Multidimensional Indexes and Rankings — 9
3. Football Development Index: Dimensions and Indicators — 27
4. Calculation Model — 37
5. Football Development Report 2013 — 47
6. Dependence between Football Rankings and Socioeconomic Indicators — 63

Conclusion — 77

Appendix A: "On-Pitch Performance" Dimension Results — 81

Appendix B: "Popularity" Dimensions Results — 87

Appendix C: "Environment" Dimensions Results — 93

Appendix D: Football Development Index Results — 101

Bibliography — 107

Index — 121

About the Authors — 123

Abbreviations

AFC	Asian Football Confederation
CAF	Confederation of African Football
CAGR	Compound Annual Growth Rate
CONCACAF	Confederation of North, Central American and Caribbean Association Football
CONMEBOL	The South American Football Confederation
EI	Education Index
FDI	Football Development Index
FIFA	Federation of International Football Federations
HDI	Human Development Index
II	Income Index
LEI	Life Expectancy Index
OFC	Oceanian Football Confederation
UEFA	Union of European Football Associations
GDP	Gross Domestic Product
CL	Champions League
UN	United Nations
WC	World Cup
NA	National Football Association

Acknowledgments

The authors would like to express their sincerest gratitude to the Rector of the Plekhanov Russian University of Economics (PRUE), Prof. V. Grishin, for providing this research with sufficient funding and moral support. A great deal of help was also provided by Prof. E. Zarova in consulting and helping form the final calculation model of the Football Development Index (FDI). This project would not be possible without the dedicated assistance from students of PRUE: K. Remizov, K. Rubanovich, A. Prilepkin, A. Shamarin, and V. Zhulevich. A great deal of time and effort was put into the visualization of the FDI methodology and results by the immensely talented V. Rozin and M. Kostin of IntellSoft Business Group.

Introduction

The statutes of the International Federation of Football Associations (FIFA), global football's governing body, clearly specify that one of the organization's main objectives is "to improve the game of football constantly and promote it globally in the light of its unifying, educational, cultural and humanitarian values, particularly through youth and development programs" (FIFA, 2015). Eisenberg (2006) established that FIFA has become an international nongovernmental organization (INGO) with its influence going beyond the conventional realms of a typical governing sports body. FIFA unites 211[1] member-countries—a number which surpasses the sum of all members in most sports organization and even in the United Nations (UN). The recognized national football associations (FAs) are spread across six continents, each with its own governing continental federation: AFC in Asia, CAF in Africa, CONCACAF in North America, CONMEBOL in South America, OFC in Oceania, and UEFA in Europe.

National associations promote their own development strategies and programs, which set the long-term goals to be achieved by the local football community. However, most of the time we hear of the failures of such initiatives, motivated by insufficient funding, mismanagement of resources, internal governance conflicts, or some other circumstances. More specific cases include Northern Ireland (Bainer, 2004), and the East African nations of Kenya, Uganda, and Tanzania (Njororai, 2017). The indication of these failures comes too late for policy-makers to be able to timely analyze these mishaps and make appropriate corrections. Similar to when corporate executives receiving the financial statement at the end of a fiscal year and being blindsided by the fact that their company is close to going bankrupt, football stakeholders can receive the news that their national football system is close to collapsing, although everything seemed fine just yesterday. Vail (2007) noticed that most sport development strategies are designed from the top down, meaning that top executives have their own vision reading the long-term prospects of the organization. This vision is then formed into a set of strategic initiatives by the mid-level management (according to their understanding of the "upper level" vision), which is then operationalized. This inevitably connected with strategic priorities being forcefully shifted due to managerial turnover. The lack of objective monitoring around football development practices is an obvious obstacle and threat that hampers the sustainable future development of sports.

The political turmoil experienced by FIFA in 2015 saw its highest officials step down from their posts and enormous pressure arise from the international community, which threatened both the organization's image and financial stability (Boudreaux, Karahan & Coats, 2016). The distress call was adequately answered and we can see FIFA aiming at incorporating new governance practices. Most notably, the FIFA Forward Programme was announced as one of the main catalysts of future football development within all 211 member nations. This development program will provide the global football community with access to funding in the amount of $1b within a four-year period: $1.25m to be allocated annually to the FAs and $10m—to the continental federations (FIFA, 2016a). With the number of countries recognized by FIFA totaling 211, the proposed distribution amount will surpass the $1.000m mark, which certainly raises questions about the financial viability and sensibility of the project.

There is no question that every corner of the globe deserves the right to develop football. However, it is also fair to assume that not everyone can execute this task with the same effectiveness. There can be numerous hypotheses pertaining to why some continents, regions, and countries have been able to produce a much better football development landscape. Academic literature has predominantly focused on identifying the exogenous determinants of football performance: socioeconomic levels (Hoffmann, Ging & Ramasamy, 2002; Vorobyev, Zarova, Solntsev, Osokin & Zhulevich, 2016), climatic conditions (Scelles & Andreff, 2014), ethnic and religious differentiation (Maderer, Holtbrügge & Schuster, 2014; Zerguini et al., 2008), and political stability (Leeds & Leeds, 2009). However, it is hard to perceive even on a hypothetical level that a national football association would be able to, on a significant level, directly impact one, let alone several, of the above-mentioned exogenous factors.

Therefore, it is evident that local football development should be reviewed from the perspective of which factors can actually be affected and influenced by the stakeholders of a nation's football development scene (a more detailed discussion of the topic of football development stakeholders will be provided in chapter 1). This book aims to construct a composite indicator that could be used by all members of the football family to benefit the world's most beloved game.

Chapter 1 will provide the reader with a conceptual discussion on what football development actually is. The chapter raises the following questions: How does football development differ from football performance? Are the concepts of sports development and football development similar? What are the possible dimensions of football development? How can the strategic goals of football development plans be operationalized and managed?

Chapter 2 introduces an overview of multidimensional indexes already successfully integrated into the strategic policy-making process of various renowned international organizations, such as the United Nations, Organization for Economic Cooperation and Development (OECD), the World Economic Forum, the International Monetary Fund (IMF), and national and regional governments. This chapter will review the history behind the conceptualization of multidimensional indexes and their subsequent approval from both academic scholars and policy-makers. Multidimensional indexes are currently widely applied in assessing socioeconomic phenomena, since these aspects cannot be easily comprehended via a single indicator (Santos & Santos, 2014). The chapter will:

- analyze the calculation specifications, historical backgrounds as well as the practical applications of several socioeconomic indexes;
- review the currently adopted index/ranking systems by various sports federations;
- assess the strategic potential of designing a composite indicator of football development.

Chapter 3 will go further on the conceptual discussion of football development as well as its dimensions. More precisely, this chapter provides an overview on the possible indicators that can be used as proxies for assessing the determinants of football development from a quantitative perspective.

Chapter 4 describes the details of calculation model of the Football Development Index based on the framework proposed by Nardo et al. (2008). Specifically, the chapter will take the reader through the statistical procedures conducted by the authors to estimate the compatibility of the selected data panel, and select the optimal normalization, weighting, and aggregation methods. An important part of the chapter is the explanation of the benchmarking process using the results of the FDI and comparing them with socioeconomic variables.

Chapter 5 will produce the results of the Football Development Index calculated using data from 2014. This chapter will provide readers with graphic illustrations of the overall index using various visualization techniques.

A breakdown of the best football development practices will also be presented for each of the six continental federations as well as for nations with similar socioeconomic characteristics.

Chapter 6 will test the causal relationships between endogenous football development factors, which will be represented via FDI values and various socioeconomic indicators. The goal of this chapter is to assess whether the Football Development Index is a more adequate indicator of football development rather than other index/ranking systems used in global football.

NOTE

1. Since May 2016 FIFA now comprises 211 members after Kosovo and Gibraltar joined the organization. However, the research was conducted prior to this decision and therefore the paper will refer to the number of FIFA-member nations as 209.

Chapter 1

Conceptualization of Football Development

According to Nardo et al. (2008), the construction of a composite indicator demands a clear understanding of:

a. the concept it is attempting to measure;
b. how will it contribute to the improvement of this aspect; and
c. who will be the main benefactors.

We often talk about football development as if the concept is thoroughly and rigorously defined. However, a review of academic literature indicated that no study has ever attempted to introduce a conceptual framework on football development. More so, it still remains unclear what dimensions and factors does it include and how can we measure it. Previously published papers have been stressing the importance of football performance. Academic literature on management, for example, Otley (1999), classifies performance as a concept comprising mainly two key aspects: efficiency (the ability to produce maximum output with the designated input) and effectiveness (the ability to achieve previously set out goals). However, the term "football performance" has not been given any particular association with its managerial "namesake" by the scientific community.

FOOTBALL PERFORMANCE

Rösch et al. (2000) define physical condition as well as technical and tactical performance as constituents of football performance. Houston and Wilson (2002) used the FIFA/Coca-Cola points of the male national teams as a proxy for football performance. A similar approach was adopted by Vorobyev et al.

(2016) for evaluating the impact of socioeconomic development on on-pitch results.

Academic scholars have also attempted to assess sports organizations from the perspective of their organizational performance (Bayle, 1999; Bayle & Madella, 2002; Bayle & Robinson, 2007; Chelladurai et al., 1987; Frisby, 1986; Madella et al., 2005; Winand et al., 2010; Winand et al., 2011) as well as corporate governance (Forster, 2006; Henry & Lee, 2004; Holt, 2006; Shilbury, Ferkins & Smythe, 2013; Ter, Gammelsæter & Senaux, 2011). A clear distinction between the two concepts is that governance can be described as a set of mechanisms that influence the decision-making process when there is a rift between ownership and control (Larcker, Richardson & Tuna, 2007), while organizational performance is the combination of an organization's ability to maximize outputs and achieve its goals (Ostroff & Schmitt, 1993). For a more thorough review of the concept of governance within the sport context we refer the reader to Ferkins, Shilbury and McDonald (2005) as well as Gammelsæter and Senaux (2013).

Henry and Lee (2004) present three interrelated approaches to help understand sport governance: systemic governance, political (or democratic) governance, and corporate (or organizational) governance. However, the authors explicitly note that their methodology provides means for resolving unethical or socially unexpected behaviors such as racism, discrimination, or conservatism, without emphasizing on sporting results or development. Andrikopoulos and Kaimenakis (2009) proposed the Football Organization Index—a composite indicator of organizational performance. Although promoting a multidimensional approach toward evaluating football entities, the authors still emphasize that their indicator is centered in the athletic performance of a football club. A more recent paper by Plumley, Wilson, and Ramchandani (2017) attempted to apply the concept of "holistic performance" in respect of professional football clubs using an experimental performance assessment model (ExPAM). Referring to the on-field/off-field dichotomy suggested by Chadwick (2009) the authors proposed to measure both financial and sporting performance of football clubs, giving equal importance to both dimensions. However, no methodological explanation was given by the authors in terms of allocating the respective weights of the selected indicators and dimensions. A somewhat similar from a conceptual standpoint but more methodologically sophisticated framework was proposed by Teodor and Adrian (2015).

Papadimitriou and Taylor (2000) attempted to assess the effectiveness of Hellenic National Sports organizations using a Multiple Constituency Approach. Similar studies were conducted for evaluating the effectiveness of national sports organizations (NSOs) in Canada (Chelladurai and Haggerty, 1991), France (Bayle and Madella, 2002), Australia (Shilbury and Moore 2006), Belgium (Winand et al., 2010), and Singapore (Koh-Tan, 2011).

These studies emphasized a multidimensional approach toward assessing sports organizations. Such an approach is more than justified due to the specific management features within sport organizations, for example, balancing financial and nonfinancial activities (Winand et al., 2010), promoting elite-level and grassroots sports (Green, 2007), engaging with both national and international umbrella organizations (Levermore, 2009), and controlling regional "networks" (Bayle & Madella, 2007).

More evidently, the above-mentioned papers review only issues related to governance and sporting performance of NSOs and professional clubs, giving little or no attention to their contribution to sports development. It seems that the best way to identify what football development actually is will be to analyze the conceptual framework on sports development.

DEFINING FOOTBALL DEVELOPMENT

Kruse (2006) refers to the concept of "sport-for-development" as being rather vague and open to several interpretations. Coalter (2010) notes that sports have always had a mythopoetic status, meaning that there are no definitive criteria for identifying the concept. Houlihan and Green (2011) conducted a thorough review of the several attempts of defining sports development. The authors note that initial view on sports development overemphasized the importance of sport in "sports development" by saying that it is about "getting more people to play more sport," while nonsport objectives were not given any regard (Houlihan & Green, 2011, 3). Collins (1995, 21) suggested that sports development is "a process whereby effective opportunities, processes, systems and structures are set up to enable and encourage people in all or particular groups and areas to take part in sport and recreation or to improve their performance to whatever level they desire."

Houlihan and Green (2011, 4) note that "sports development is highly contested in terms of objectives (which range from talent identification and development, through enhanced health to moral improvement), practices (ranging from the development of sport-specific technical skills to recreational 'fun days') and practitioners (ranging from career sports development officers and coaches to youth workers and religious missionaries)." Hylton and Bramham (2008) highlight sports development as an inclusive process which engages the broadest array of policy-makers, agencies, organizations, practitioners, and participants. According to the authors, sports development simultaneously grasps various interrelated aspects: mass participation, social inclusion, talent development, elite performance, and contribution to wider educational, social, and economic policies and practices. Therefore, according to the authors, sport development describes the policies, processes, and practices that are aimed at providing "sporting opportunities and positive sporting experiences." The important and contentious area facing sports development has been the need to work at both grassroots levels and elite sport. This statement confirms our a priori assumptions that football performance (i.e., elite-sport results) can only be regarded as a sub-dimension of football development. This is further supported by academic research (e.g., Green, 2006; Grix & Carmichael, 2012), which says that elite sport is seen by major stakeholders as the sole proxy for overall sport development, simply because it is the "usual suspect." This is exactly why funding and efforts are disproportionally distributed between sports activities at elite and grassroots levels. However, the relationship between success at elite sports tournaments and sport participation are much less straightforward than one might assume. For more details on this topic we refer the reader to Bloom, Hughes, and Gagnon (2006), Coalter (2004), and London Research Institute (2007).

Based on the conducted review of the conceptual literature on sports development, the authors attempt to propose a definition of football development. Football development is a complex process entangling the affairs of all football stakeholders (i.e., governments, federations, clubs, players, supporters, sports, and managerial staff) in order to promote, encourage, and provide communities with the opportunities to play the game and receive positive experiences from both grassroots and elite football. With this concept in mind we will proceed with the next stage of the research—calculation methodology.

STAKEHOLDERS OF FOOTBALL DEVELOPMENT

It has been determined that football development is connected to both amateur and elite-level football. At this point it is imperative to highlight what stakeholder groups are most invested and interested in developing the game of football. According to numerous studies (Parent & Séguin, 2007; Harrison & Sayogo, 2014; Walters & Tacon, 2010), ensuring transparency among all stakeholder groups sparks increased efficiency and boosts motivation and confidence. Freeman (1984, 246) characterized the concept of stakeholder groups as being deceptively simple. Its simplicity is explained by the ease of identifying the parties that can affect or/and be affected by a certain organization or phenomenon. The deceptive nature of stakeholder groups is stipulated by the enormous difficulties connected to managing relationships with and between them. Wolfe and Putler (2002) argue the desired outcome of stakeholder management is to ensure strategic priorities are aligned with stakeholder needs. Rowley (1997) notes that stakeholder theory has predominantly relied on analytical frameworks aimed at categorizing stakeholder groups based on how they influence a firm. The following three steps were proposed by Wood (1994) for conducting stakeholder analysis:

1. Stakeholder identification (investors, management, employees, customers, suppliers, etc.)
2. Determination of stakeholder interests (financial gain, social utility, image and prestige, etc.)
3. Estimating the level of stakeholder influence and power

Wolfe and Putler (2002) have expressed their concern that in most cases the identification of stakeholders has been conducted in an arbitrary manner without a sound theoretical framework, while also little emphasis has been given to the homogeneity/heterogeneity issue within stakeholder groups. Bryson (2004) proposed a number of tools that can be used for classifying stakeholder groups. Most notably, the power vs. interest grid seemed to be a rather solid yet straightforward approach with four stakeholder groups being identified based on their levels of interest (in a political sense) and power (Table 1.1).

The power vs. interest grid is a useful tool for identifying key stakeholders, that is, who has the most power and is the most interested. The understanding of these constructs within stakeholder framework facilitates better stakeholder management. With regards to the sports industry the stakeholder still causes much debate and operational challenges (Ferkins & Shilbury, 2015). Financial constraints due to limited resources lie in the epicenter of the relationships between sports managers and stakeholders (Senaux, 2008). The multidimensional nature of sport forces the industry to pay attention to both for-profit and noncommercial organizations (Wicker & Breuer, 2011). Brown (2002) notes that although stakeholder theory derived from the commercial sector, it can easily be applied to the domain of nonprofit organizations.

Ferkins and Shilbury (2010) see the regional representatives of NSOs as the key stakeholders of the strategic governing function of the NSO. Miragaia, Ferreira, and Carreira (2014) highlight top management along with member associations and sponsors as the three main stakeholder groups included in strategic decision-making of sports organizations.

Table 1.1 Power vs. Interest Grid

		Power	
		Low	High
Interest	Low	Crowd	Context setters
	High	Subjects	Players

Source: Bryson, 2004.

Sport has been gaining increasing importance in state policy and in the affairs of international organizations, especially in the twenty-first century (Nauright, 2004). In 2002, the general secretary of the United Nations noted that sports cannot only improve the lives of individuals but whole communities. Therefore, governments were encouraged to promote sports development activities on a systematic nationwide level (Coalter, 2010). Football being a team sport as well as one of the most accessible promotes social inclusiveness and tolerance like no other (Tacon, 2007). The United Nations (2005) see participation as the cornerstone of the conceptual basis of sports. However, there is empirical evidence that some nations consider elite sport results as their number one priority.

China is a vivid example of an elite-sport oriented government. More specifically, football has been called by Xi Jin-Ping, the general secretary of the Chinese Communist Party, as the main focus point of state affairs with the new development strategy plan being put to work in order to ensure China's football dominance by "entering the World Cup," 'hosting the World Cup," and "winning the World Cup" (Tan, Huang, Bairner & Chen, 2016).

National football associations are indisputably a key stakeholder of football development since they are members of FIFA and, thus, must conform with the organization's statutes, which explicitly stress the importance of developing the game on every corner of the globe (FIFA, 2016b). Their interest in football development ought to be at its peak, since this could be regarded as one of their key success factors, which ensures their credibility. NAs along with their regional representatives are also the ones conducting the operationalization of strategic initiatives.

Football clubs and leagues can apply sufficient pressure on both international and national football organizations, mainly due to their financial capabilities and ownership of player contracts (Rohde & Breuer, 2016). The threat of a European Super League replacing the UEFA Champions League as the continent's top club football competition has been discussed in both academic and sporting communities for quite some time (Vrooman, 2007; Scelles et al., 2016; Scelles, 2017). Football clubs have become so autonomous that even FIFA is now forced to schedule mega events, such as the World Cup, in line with the needs of the clubs and their players (Gürtler, Lang & Pawlowski, 2015).

Professional athletes have an immense impact on the sports development scene, since they are the key element of the elite-sport spectacle. Their effect can largely be explained by the bargaining power. Most notably, association football was stunned by the notorious *Bosman* ruling, which changed the landscape of the European labor market (Dejonghe & Van Opstal, 2010; Szymanski, 2010). However, the interest levels of professional athletes can hardly be called strong. Most players brought up in seemingly "low" football

Table 1.2. Football Development Stakeholder Groups

Stakeholder Group	Power vs. Interest Grid	Key Stakeholder Interest in Football Development
State government	Player	Amateur (all cases) and elite level (certain cases).
National and regional football associations	Subjects/Players	Amateur (all cases) and elite level (all cases).
Professional football leagues and clubs	Context setters/players	Elite level
Professional football players	Context setters	Elite level
Amateur sports clubs	Subjects	Amateur level

Source: Created by the authors based on Bryson, 2004.

developed nations can still realize their potential through joining foreign clubs (Kleven, Landai & Saez 2013). A summarized power vs. interest grid of football development stakeholders is provided in Table 1.2.

Chapter 2
Overview of Multidimensional Indexes and Rankings

During the past decades, the question of providing a quantitative representation of the concept of development has been attracting increasing attention among academic researchers, non-governmental organizations (NGOs), and policy-makers (Santos & Santos, 2014). Measurement approaches started out as simple single-factor models solely relying on one-sided assessment of a problem (Figure 2.1). For example, during the postwar period, gross domestic product (GDP) and gross national product (GNP) averaged by a country's population were primarily if not solely regarded as valid indicators of "general development" (Hiks & Streeten, 1979). The subsequent years saw a shift in the conceptualization of development and comprehension that nonmonetary indicators must also be taken into account in the context of socioeconomic development (Santos & Santos, 2014). This leads to the creation of the portfolio measurement approach where a broader set of indicators would describe various aspects of development. The Basic Needs Approach was one of most prominent alternatives to measuring development via six dimensions: nutrition, basic education, health, sanitation, water supply and housing, and related infrastructure which would supplement GNP (Streeten, 1981).

However, the portfolio approach was proving to be complex for policy-makers to interpret the readings of each dimension. The lack of transparency of indicator portfolios prompted the development of composite indexes. Freudenberg (2003) states that, ideally, composite indicators are supposed to provide an understanding of performance beyond a single-minded approach. As early as 1960s Harbison and Myers (1964) designed an indicator for measuring human resource development. Subsequent works contributed to the formation of a whole array of composite indexes. McGranahan (1972)

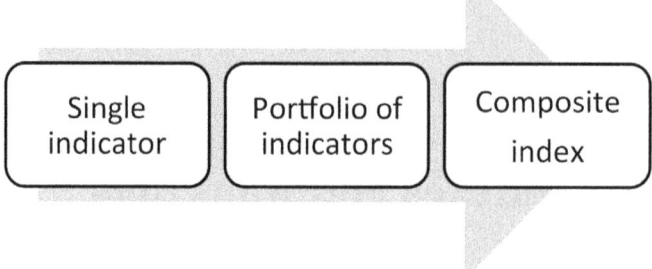

Figure 2.1 Evolution of Approaches for Measuring Development. Created by the authors, based on Santos and Santos, 2014

created an index of socioeconomic development, Morris (1978) proposed a Physical Quality of Life Index (PQLI), the portfolio Basic Needs Approach was modified into the Unsatisfied Basic Needs Index, and so forth. Composite indicators became more appealing to academic researchers, since they were able to attract far more attention from the public and affect the mindset of policy-makers with greater effectiveness and impact than a portfolio of indictors with a qualitative discussion (Streeten, 1994).

An academic report prepared by the PASTILLE Consortium (2002) concluded that composite development indexes have the following important purposes:

- Providing a conceptual understanding of the phenomenon it is attempting to measure;
- Supporting decision-making process;
- Creating a more explicit platform for stakeholder engagement where inputs and outputs are numerically represented and well-defined; and
- Resolving conflicts and strengthening relations among stakeholders.

This chapter provides an overview of currently active and globally recognized socioeconomic indexes. The indicators analyzed in the following sections of this chapter are regarded as the more sophisticated successors of the above-mentioned indexes. A review of the currently employed rating and ranking systems in sports will also be conducted by the authors in order to understand the current situation with composite indicator design within the sports industry. The chapter will be concluded with a discussion on the strategic importance of composite sports development indexes and their potential strategic role for sports policy-makers and stakeholders.

SOCIOECONOMIC APPLICATIONS

Nowadays composite indexes are the most commonly applied tool for providing a quantitative representation for socioeconomic phenomena. This tendency can be vividly observed in such areas as well-being (Benjamin, Heffetz, Kimball & Szembrot, 2014), quality of life (Schlesinger, Taulet, Alves & Burguete, 2016), and happiness (Iacus, Porro, Salini & Siletti, 2015). Globally renowned organizations, such as the United Nations, OECD, the World Economic Forum, and the IMF, are producing composite indicators in a wide variety of fields, which confirms their increasing role in policy-making. However, Streeten (1994) notes that there is certainly no index or set of indicators that would capture the full depth and richness of various socio-economic determinants (e.g., human development). Composite indexes are a useful tool for simplifying a complex problem for the purpose of ascertaining the best approaches to resolving it. This section will thoroughly review the Human Development Index, which is considered by most at the cornerstone of composite index development, while also reviewing its sister-indicator, the Multidimensional Poverty Index, the Ease of Doing Business Index, as well as the rapidly emerging Social Progress Index. The choice of analyzing these particular indexes is explained by the varying approaches to the rationale of their introduction, design (i.e., indicator and dimension selection, aggregation, robustness), as well as their differing practical applications.

Human Development Index

Though the socioeconomic indexes mentioned in the introductory part of this chapter contributed greatly to the methodological and theoretical aspects of assessing the complex phenomenon of development, they were not perceived by policy-makers as practical tools to support decision-making. It was not until 1990 when the first Human Development Report (HDR) was published that composite indicators really received their well-deserved exposure. The initial HDR identified that "development is much more than just the expansion of income and wealth" and defined human development as "the process of enlarging people's choices" (UNDP, 1990, 10). The HDR was centered on the newly introduced Human Development Index (HDI), which comprised sub-indexes that measure income, health, and education levels. The HDI was created by Mahbub ul Haq based on the previous research of Sen (1979, 1983, 1988). The primary difference between the HDI and previously designed socioeconomic indexes was the shift from assessing the means of development toward evaluating the opportunities that people have to develop (Santos & Santos, 2014). Anand and Sen (1994) formed the initial methodology of the HDI, which included GDP per capita (PPP) as an indicator of living standards, life expectancy at birth as a determinant of healthcare levels, and literacy rate as a proxy for the country's education levels. However,

The HDI was able to include a strictly economic indicator (GDP per capita and later GNI per capita), while also giving similar importance to adequate social development factors. The relative simplicity in calculation (i.e., the arithmetic mean of the normalized data on the three indicators) and the small amount of components made the HDI very attractive both to policy-makers and the public since it was both easy to interpret and transparent. The HDI today, though slightly modified in its calculation methodology, is still a relevant indicator of assessing modern socioeconomic development and continues to be a valuable component of the United Nations (UN) HDR. The number of produced UN HDRs now surpasses 25. The substantial amount of collected data through the years has provided policy-makers with the opportunity of conducting trend analyses (e.g., year-on-year growth rates) as well as inter-country comparisons, since the nations included in the HDR also form a unified ranking based on their HDI scores.

With its core principles and goals remaining intact the HDI has experienced several methodological changes over the years that were triggered by criticism to the:

a. dimensions of development covered by the index;
b. implicit trade-offs between the dimensions;
c. absence of attention to population distribution inequality; and
d. statistical inconsistency.

(a) McGillivray (1991) was the first to notice that the three dimensions of the HDI are highly correlated. This raises the question of the validity of the particular selection of variables. Comparing cross-country development based on one of the HDI component would produce similar results to those presenting the overall index itself. Indeed, Nardo et al. (2008) recommend including only insignificantly correlated indicators in order to exclude data overlapping.

Sagar and Najam (1998) criticize the HDI due to its negligence toward environmental issues and the "relationships between the performance of countries on the environmental and human development dimensions." Bravo (2014) proposed to "amend" the HDI by introducing a Human Sustainable Development Index (HSDI), which would, apart from education, healthcare, and income, incorporate an environmental dimension.

In the more relevant work of Ravallion (2012) it is noted that since 2010 the HDI has replaced several indicators. For instance, income is now measured through Gross National Income (GNI) rather than GDP and education is represented via mean years of schooling and the expected years of schooling (Table 2.1).

Table 2.1 **Dimensions and Indicators of the Human Development Index from 2010**

Dimension	Proxy Indicator	Weight
Education	Mean years of schooling	1/6
	Expected years of schooling	1/6
Health	Life expectancy at birth	1/3
Income	Gross National Income (GNI per capita)	1/3

Source: (UNDP, 2010).

(b) The HDI uses a simple weighting method where every dimension is allocated equal importance. Therefore, according to the HDI methodology, each of the three sub-indexes (i.e., Education Index, Life Expectancy Index, and Income Index) not only have the same effect on the overall level of human development, but can also be equally substituted. The fact that the HDI uses an equal weighting method can be mainly explained by the wish of ul Haq to make the index more appealing to policy-makers and the general public through a simple calculation model. However, one of the main aspects of contracting valid composite indicators is the explicit nature of the trade-offs that are made between the key dimensions through setting weights. The employment of an arbitrary/equal method only facilitates the implicitness of the HDI theoretical framework (Decancq & Lugo, 2013).

It has to be noted that the majority of the research papers that attempted to propose a more sophisticated weighting method for the HDI concluded that equal importance of all three dimensions is a fairly justified trade-off. Therefore, the main shortcoming of the HDI methodology was not the incorporation of equal weights themselves but merely the lack of objectification given to this choice.

(c) Streeten (1994) stated that the inclusion of per capita income can conceal great inequalities. While sharing these concerns, Chatterjee (2005) proposed an alternative measure of human development, since he believed that the HDI ignored the extent of inequality in quality of life over the members of population. He introduced an index of uptilt that would account for the distribution of quality of life among urban and rural residents.

(d) Noorbakhsh (1998) criticized the mini-max normalization method used in the HDI calculation model. The author was concerned that overall index could be sensitive to the fixed values of F_{min} and F_{max} of each dimension. The UNDP justifies the "fixed" approach by stating the extreme values were selected via observation "over a long period"; however, no specification of the precise timeframe is provided. Furthermore, the somewhat arbitrary selection of extreme values for each component results in their different scaling. Such a fact introduces unintentional weighting, since the normalized mean value would most likely vary across all three dimensions. An alternative

Table 2.2 Evolution of HDI Calculation Methodology from 1990–2010

Year	Value Range for Normalization Procedure		Indicators			Aggregation
	Min	Max	Health	Education	Income	
1990	Observed		Life expectancy at birth	Adult (25+ years) literacy rate	Logged real GDP per capita (PPP)	Arithmetic mean with equal weights
1991–1993					Atkinson formula adjusted real GDP per capita (PPP)	
1994	Fixed			(2/3) Adult literacy rate index; (1/3) Mean years of schooling		
1995–1998				(2/3) Adult literacy rate index; (1/3) Combined gross enrollment ratio index with a cap starting to bind in 1996		
1999				(2/3) Adult (15+) literacy rate index; (1/3) Combined gross enrollment ratio index with a cap starting to bind in 1996	Logged real GDP per capita (PPP)	
2000–2009						
2010	Fixed	Observed		(1/2) Mean years of schooling index; (1/2) Expected years of schooling index	Real GNI per capita (PPP) with natural logarithmic transformation	Geometric mean with equal weights

Source: Based on Klugman, Rodríguez, and Choi, 2011.

would be to use standardization (z-scores) to reduce the mean value of each indicator to 0 and the standard deviation to 1. See Table 2.2 for a summarized overview of the methodological changes of the HDI.

The introduction of the HDI was merely a stepping-stone of the composite indicator framework, which went on cover issues such as gender equality—the Gender-Related Development Index (GDI) and the Gender Empowerment Measure (GEM) were developed in 1995; human poverty through the Human Poverty Index (HPI), published in the 1997 HDR, which was later substituted by the Multidimensional Poverty Index (MPI); as well as many more socioeconomic aspects. The following narrative of the chapter will focus on "younger" index methodologies in order to ascertain the current trends of the composite indicator framework.

Multidimensional Poverty Index

The issue of poverty has been covered in every publication of the HDR starting from 1997, when the HPI was introduced. The MPI, the successor of the HPI, was initially included in the 2010 HDR. The methodological enhancements proposed by the 2010 HDR, which also significantly changed the methodology of the HDI, were based on:

a. Previous academic literature, confirming the presence of cause-effect relationships between dimension and factors;
b. The enduring consensus both on issues of human rights and the Millennium Development Goals (MDGs);
c. Philosophical and psychological accounts on the basics of human rights;
d. Availability of sufficient and trustworthy data.

Data has always been the constraint that hampered methodological breakthroughs in composite index development. As more information on global human development became available, the methodology of the Human Development Index became more complex, while also contributing to the design of new assessment tools, such as the MPI. Alkire and Santos (2010) were the "masterminds" behind the MPI methodology and state that although sufficient academic literature criticizes the absence of several key factors (e.g., human rights) in both the HDI and the previous HPI, it is currently impossible to incorporate these suggestions since no reliable data for 100+ developed countries can be obtained.

At the present time the MPI is used to assess three dimensions of the human development, mirroring the components of the HDI: health, education, and living standard. However, the MPI uses a broader set of factors (see Figure 2.2).

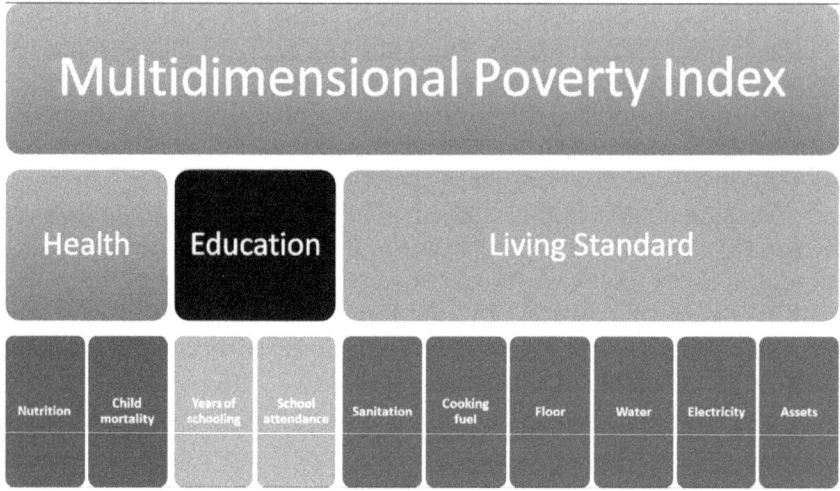

Figure 2.2 Dimensions and Indicators of MPI. Created by the authors based on UNDP, 2010

Ten indicators in total are used by the UNDP to assess multidimensional poverty, six of which represent the Living Standard dimension, while the other four are equally distributed among the remaining two dimensions. The criteria for indicator selection were made explicitly simple: the indicators needed to be internationally comparable while also being reliable. For a more detailed discussion on the selection of the MPI indicators see Alkire and Eli (2010).

From a methodological standpoint the MPI adopts a similar weighting approach that is used in the HDI. Alkire and Santos (2010) explicitly allocate equal weights to each of the three dimensions as well as equally weighting the indicators within each dimension. However, the authors note that the effective weight of the Living Standard dimension will tend to be higher, since it contributes more to poverty in poor countries. The aggregation procedure is based on the Alkire-Foster method (Alkire & Foster, 2011), which uses the Adjusted Headcount Ratio. The method can be only applied to ordinal data and identifies the breadth of multiple deprivations of the poor. The MPI comprises two sub-indexes: the first is used to evaluate proportion of population experiencing multiple deprivations, while the second sub-index measures deprivation intensity. Alkire, Roche, Seth, and Sumner (2015) proposed three approaches to presenting the large dataset of the MPI. Their solution focused on identifying the poorest billion population in order to answer the question, "where do the poorest live?" The authors grouped the "billion" by geographical characteristics (i.e., poorest countries); however, it did not fully account for the deprivation variance of each region, so classification based on poorest subnational regions was introduced. The third approach used individual poverty profiles. Apart from global rankings the MPI can also be used to construct continental, national, and subnational rankings.

A paper published by Angulo, Díaz and Pardo (2016) proposed to slightly modify the MPI methodology proposed by Alkire and Foster (2011) to form a nation-specific multidimensional poverty measurement labeled as the "Colombian Multidimensional Poverty Index" (CMPI). Notably, the authors attempted to introduce a more elaborate weighting method; however, data-driven approaches proved to be incompatible with multidimensional measurement. Therefore the equal weighting method was retained. The set of indicators included in the MPI was slightly altered so that the CMPI could better incorporate regional peculiarities. The authors conducted a review of literature on key dimensions usually adopted for assessing socioeconomic phenomena in Colombia, analyzed the most frequently used indexes in South America, and aligned the indicators with the core values of the nation's constitution, the government's social policy. CMPI was also proposed as a tool for monitoring the achievement of poverty reduction strategies established by the country's National Development Plan.

Ease of Doing Business Index

The World Bank annually publishes the Doing Business—a report set to evaluate the global business environment. One of the key components of this report is the Ease of Doing Business Index (EDBI)[1]. The indicator employs a set of 41 indicators covering 10 areas of business relations: starting a business, dealing with construction permits, getting electricity, registering property, getting credit, protecting minority investors, paying taxes, trading across borders, enforcing contracts, and resolving insolvency. Based on the EDBI a global Ease of Doing Business Ranking is formed covering approximately 180 countries (Pinheiro-Alves & Zambujal-Oliveira, 2012). The calculation methodology of the index is pretty straightforward as well, since every indicator is allocated an equal weight and aggregated via an arithmetic mean.

Pinheiro-Alves and Zambujal-Oliveira (2012), following the recommendations of Nardo et al. (2008), conducted a multivariate analysis to test the reliability of the EDBI. Factor Analysis and Cronbach's alpha were used to analyze the correlation between the variables as well as to verify the adequate structure of the index. The authors were able to establish that the index lacks robustness and exposed its high heterogeneity. Ninety percent of the variance of 9 out of 10 EDBI groups is explained by one or two indicators within each group.

Though the EDBI exhibits some serious methodological flaws, it remains an important determinant of a country's investment attractiveness and mainly its ability to attract foreign direct investment. Djankov et al. (2006) were able to establish that the 2004 Ease of Doing Business Ranking significantly influenced GDP growth. Jayasuriya (2011) used panel data of 84 nations from 2006 to 2009 and was able to establish that a higher EDBI is likely to increase FDI inflow. Canare, Ang, and Mendoza (2014) applied the EDBI as the sole indicator to form recommendations on the future reforms regarding the establishment of a more lenient business environment in APEC countries.

Social Progress Index

The Social Progress Index (SPI) is the "youngest" composite indicator included in our review with its initial introduction dating back to 2013. The SPI defines social progress as the "capacity of a society to meet the basic human needs of its citizens, establish the building blocks that allow citizens and communities to enhance and sustain the quality of their lives, and create the conditions for all individuals to reach their full potential" (Social Progress Imperative, 2016). The authors of the SPI also emphasize the exclusive use of outcome indicators rather than input measures. This is explained by the fact that for an "input" index to work a consensual understanding about the cause-effect relationships between inputs and outcomes is needed (Fleurbaey & Blanchet, 2013). The SPI focuses explicitly on noneconomic factors by adopting the "Beyond GDP" approach, which can be traced to the works of Costanza et al. (2009), Fleurbaey (2009), Fleurbaey and Blanchet (2013), and Kubiszewski et al. (2013).The SPI also covers a triad of dimensions: basic human needs, foundations of well-being, and opportunity with four components each (see Table 2.3).

Each of the four components within the three dimensions is equally weighted. However, each component includes several indicators, the weights of which were measured using principal component analysis (PCA). The results of PCA weighting were almost equivalent to the values of equal weighting, although it allows to account for the difference in data availability and indicator divergence. The selection of indicators for each component is based on whether it (a) is adequately calculated to provide an adequate representation of the assessed phenomenon; (b) is publicly available, which ensures transparency and independency from intentional overestimation; and (c) covers a substantial number (if not all) nations included in the index. A total of 53 indicators were used for the 2016 version of the SPI. The temporal scope of the 2016 SPI varies from 2005 to 2016 with the "average" time period of the data being the year of 2014. Not every nation is represented in the SPI, the cutoff was made when a country had a single missing value in more than three components. The missing values were recovered using regression-based imputation.

Table 2.3 Social Progress Index Structure

Social Progress Index		
Basic Human needs	Foundations of Well-Being	Opportunity
Nutrition and Basic Medical Care	Access to Basic Knowledge	Personal Rights
Water and Sanitation	Access to Information and Communications	Personal Freedom and Choice
Shelter	Health and Wellness	Tolerance and Inclusion
Personal Safety	Environmental Quality	Access to Advanced Education

Source: Social Progress Imperative (2016).

Data normalization was conducted using an approach, which was labeled as the "best-worst case" score, but in essence is the mini-max method, which is also adopted by the HDI. Indicator aggregation to calculate each component score is performed by simply summing the weighted scores. The subsequent aggregation of components into dimensions and the dimensions into the overall SPI is also achieved through summing the weighted scores.

One of the main innovations of the SPI is the introduction of an explicit benchmarking tool, where it does not simply cross-analyze country data on an absolute basis, but looks at the relative strengths and weaknesses of nations. Such an approach allows to determine the performance of nations compared to countries with similar income-level countries. Nations are classified into groups of 15 using a four-year average GDP (PPP) per capita. Once the groups are defined a country's SPI score is compared to the media value within the group. If country's score exceeds the absolute deviation from the median value within the groups, then it is classified as an "over performer," if it is lower than the absolute deviation—the country is an underperformer.

Pate and Sweo (2016) highlight the transparency of the SPI as one of its main merits, since only open-source data is used. This allows companies to comprehend not only the value of the overall SPI but also its components when making investment and other business-related decisions. After analyzing three different cases of companies from significantly differing markets and with varying strategic goals the authors were able to conclude that the SPI is a valuable tool for determining country site selections.

The SPI has been gaining a fair amount of attention from policy-makers, most notably in South America. Brazil, Chile, Argentina, Peru, Colombia, Paraguay, and Bolivia are currently using the SPI methodology on national, regional, and municipal scales. An increasing interest to the project has also been circulating in Central America and Europe. An interesting feature of the SPI is how it is adapted at regional, subnational, and city level. Due to the obvious discrepancies between data collection, reporting procedures, and other factors it is highly unlikely to ensure that indicators adopted by the global SPI can be applied at "lower" geographical scales. The solution introduced by the Social Progress Initiative suggested that the core framework of the index (dimensions and component) must remain constant irrespective of the region where it is being applied, but the indictors, which are basically quantitative proxies for the components and dimensions, can be selected individually as long as their conceptual basis remains in line with the mission of the SPI.

RANKINGS IN SPORTS

Measurement systems in sports provide a much less elaborate methodological framework and have a lower strategic impact on policy-making. Sport rankings are predominantly applied to rate teams and athletes based on previous relevant results in order to establish the competitive prospect for a particular tournament. In the case of football, rankings are used to avoid drawing strong teams/athletes in the early competition stages. This sort of approach is justified by the increased commercial interests of the sports industry, since latter tournament stages are expected to produce higher quality match-ups and, thus, consumers will be more inclined to pay "top dollar" for such a spectacle. Sports rankings also serve as somewhat indicators of athletic quality of both teams and athletes. For example, The Football Association (England's governing football body) uses the position of a player's national team in the FIFA/Coca-Cola Ranking to determine whether or not he deserves to be given a work permit to play professional football on English soil.

The first systemic review of global rating systems in sports was conducted by Stefani (1997). The author was able to establish a general pattern of sports rating systems, which comprised three calculation phases (Table 2.4). Therefore, sports rankings represented much less sophisticated and statistically robust methodologies than those used in socioeconomic indexes and recommended by the OECD (Nardo et al., 2008).

In his later work, Stefani (2011) reviewed nearly 100 rating systems from 159 international sports federations. As a result the author introduced a taxonomy of global sports rating systems: subjective, accumulative, and adjustive. Subjective systems were used in combat sports (i.e., kickboxing, mixed martial arts) and were based on expert opinions about the physical and technical form of a particular athlete. Accumulative systems proposed to combine points for each competition, which motivated athletes to enter as many competitions as possible (e.g., tennis). Adjustive systems incorporate probability-based predictions to objectify the ranking (e.g., chess).

Overview of Multidimensional Indexes and Rankings

Table 2.4 Phases of Sports Rating Calculation

Phase	Procedure
1	Sporting results are weighted to form contingent points for each competition
2	Contingent points are summed up to provide a season value
3*	Seasonal values are combined to construct a ratio

Source: Stefani (1997).
*This step may be redundant if the rating includes only the results of a single season.

A more relevant and substantial overview of various evaluation systems in several socioeconomic areas, including sports, was conducted by Karminsky and Polozov (2016). Their analysis covered a broad array of sports from globally popular varieties such as football and tennis to intellectual games such as Go. Lasek, Szlávik, and Bhulai (2013) reviewed a distinct number of international sports ranking methodologies starting from the well-known FIFA/Coca-Cola Ranking to the far more sophisticated Markovian and Network-based ranking systems. The authors tested the predictive power of various rating models to determine whether the measurements can actually provide an adequate representation of a country's current athletic form. The results showed that nations were able to frequently outperform their ranking position in the less sophisticated rating systems (e.g., the male FIFA/Coca-Cola Ranking), meaning that their predictive capabilities were relatively low. The best scores were acquired via the Elo rating. An overview of these rating methods will be provided later in this chapter.

Male FIFA/Coca-Cola Ranking

In August 1993 FIFA introduced the first edition of the ranking of on-pitch results of male national A-teams. At that time the ranking methodology represented a simple arithmetic formula of summing up points from game results: 3 points per victory and 1 point in the case of a draw. During that period of time it was the fact of the existence of a rating system which was the most important accomplishment rather than the peculiarities of the ranking methodology itself (Gásquez & Royuela, 2014).

FIFA understood that rating methodologies must serve as an additional incentive for all National Football Associations to improve the on-pitch performance of their teams. In addition, the FIFA Rankings were the first official demonstration of the distribution of global football supremacy. The FIFA ranking system evolved during the years, proposing more elaborate approaches to presenting a country's football supremacy. New support factors were added, and the methodology became more complex. For additional motivation, FIFA introduced two nominations based on the results of countries according to the ranking:

- Team of the year—a title which is given to the number 1 national squad according to the ranking;
- Best mover of the year—an award implemented to commemorate countries which have shown the most spectacular progress through the ranks.

The most recent FIFA ranking methodology was approved and finalized in 2006. This methodology takes into account all international matches (both official and friendly games), the country's confederation affiliation, the opposing team's strength (via its FIFA ranking), the amount of goals scored, and the game's level of importance. The calculations are conducted using the following formula:

$$P = M \times I \times T \times C \qquad (2.1)$$

Where M—match outcome,[2]
I—match importance,[3]
T—opposing team skill coefficient,[4]
C—confederation coefficient of the playing team[5]

In addition to the official FIFA/Coca-Cola Ranking there are other methodologies focused on rating football entities. For instance, the World Elo Rating System is the most commonly used in intellectual games (Bootsma & Bhulai, 2015). One of this rating system's distinctive characteristics is the presence of a match predicting equation, which updates each country's rank based on the comparison between the expected and actual results. The World Football Elo Rating System only includes the results of male senior A-teams. However, the methodology of the official FIFA Women's World Ranking is considered to be a variation of the Elo rating system.

FIFA Women's World Ranking

Surprisingly, FIFA uses varying methodologies to rate male and female national team results. The Women's ranking is updated after each match and adopts the following formula:

$$R'_i = R_i + K(O_i - P_i) \qquad (2.2)$$

R'_i—the rating of an *i*-country after the match;
R_i—the rating of an *i*-country before the match;
K—the match significance multiplier;
O_i—the actual outcome of an *i*-nation's match;
P_i—the predicted outcome of an *i*-nation's match.

The Women's ranking presents a more complicated ranking procedure, since it includes a match prediction variable (P_i), which attributes this ranking methodology to the category of Elo rating systems. For further details on the FIFA Women's World Ranking we refer the reader to the official methodology.[6]

As noted before, FIFA conducts rankings of both male and female national teams. The main shortcoming of the women's ranking is that it includes only 139 out of 209 FIFA-member countries which points out an insufficient amount of popularity among women's football. At the same time the women's ranking possesses the same flaws as the men's ranking (Jacobs, 2014).

Football Club Rankings

At the moment no unified global approach toward evaluating football club performance exists. However, some continental football federations calculate their own rankings of countries based on the sporting results of their club representatives using different ranking methods.

The Union of European Football Associations (UEFA) regularly updates and publishes its club ranking on the official website (UEFA, 2015). The Asian Football Confederation (AFC) also has its own system of scoring club performance of NAs, which uses a 70-point rating scale. Unlike UEFA, where national team and club rankings are calculated separately and do not depend on one another, the AFC club ranking is a component of the overall Asian Football Associations ranking which incorporates both club and national team results (AFC, 2014). The AFC ranking incorporates the following guidelines for allocating scores:

- For every victory 3 points are awarded, in the case of a draw—1 point, a loss—0 point;
- During the play-off stage points are given for progressing into the next stage of the tournament. Each stage progression is valued at 3 points;
- The overall sum of acquired points by a National FA is then divided by the number of club representatives which have participated in the tournament during the season;
- Points acquired in the second tier club competition (The AFC Cup) are divided by 3.

The Confederation of African Football (CAF) uses its own five-year club ranking (CAF, 2014). The rating is conducted using a methodology showcased in Table 2.5, where the amount of points awarded after the finish of tournament stage is displayed.

Table 2.5 CAF Club Ranking Method

Stage	Tournament — CAF Champions League (Top tier)	CAF Cup (2nd tier)
Winner	5	4
Runner-up	4	3
Semifinalist	3	2
3rd place in group	2	1
4th place in group	1	1

Source: based on Global Football Ranks (2017).

The number of acquired points is multiplied by the weight awarded to every season of the tournaments during a five-year period (with the highest weight given to the latest edition of the competitions). In this case, if we assume that the 2014 season is the latest edition of the tournament, then the 2014 season is multiplied by 5, 2013 season by 4, 2012 season by 3, 2011 season by 2, 2010 season by 1. The other continental federations (Oceania, North America, and South America) do not conduct such rankings.

STRATEGIC POTENTIAL OF SPORTS DEVELOPMENT RANKINGS

The review of the socioeconomic application of composite indicators provided us with valuable insight into both methodological peculiarities and their strategic importance to policy-makers. Sports rankings, however, have proven to be solely focused on the competitive side of sports, while being reluctant toward establishing long-term sustainable growth and development. It is highly unlikely to get a clear and undisputable global overview of the football scenery through the results of a single national team. FIFA-sanctioned tournaments aside from the Men's World Cup include various age groups starting from the under-17 level, beach football competitions, and futsal tournaments. Continental club rankings either adopt unimpressive and substantially varying methodological approaches, or do not rate club performance at all. The inexistence of a globally accepted measurement system that would include the key development aspect of football from grassroots participation to elite performance seriously undermines the efforts of both FIFA and its continental federations to achieve strategic milestones.

The necessity of introducing a development index in sports is also dictated by the staggering member quorums of some international federations, which may even surpass the number of nations recognized by the United Nations (see Table 2.6).[7]

Table 2.6 List of the World's Largest Single-Sport Federations

Rank	Sport	International Federation	Number of member countries
	Table tennis	ITTF	226
	Volleyball	FIVB	221
	Basketball	FIBA	215
	Athletics	IAAF	214
	Tennis	ITF	211
	Football	FIFA	211
	Aquatic sports	FINA	207
	Handball	IHF	204
	Boxing (amateur)	AIBA	200
	Chess	FIDE	188

Source: Created by the authors based on ITTF (2017), FIVB (2017), IAAF (2017), FIBA (2017), FIFA (2017), ITF (2017), FINA (2017), IHF (2017), AIBA (2017), FIDE (2017).

Based on the conducted review of socioeconomic indexes it is evident that a sports development index could have a number of important practical applications:

1. *Establishing and scaling critical success factors*

Policy-makers/governments, which view sports as an important aspect of their social well-being and a determinant of national identity, as well national football associations (NAs) could use the methodology of the Football Development Index (FDI) to set long-term goals. Therefore, the FDI can help decision-makers focus on both the "means" and "ends" of football development by incorporating its critical success factors. These factors may in future serve as strategic goals set out by national football stakeholders and be incorporated in their development programs.

2. *Benchmarking tool*

The index could be used to determine the global best practices of football development, which can then be adopted by other NAs. By grouping nations with similar socioeconomic, demographic, geographic, and other characteristics we can establish particular success' patterns relevant to countries with particular attributes.

3. *Monitoring and objectifying financial allocation*

The above-mentioned FIFA Forward Programme is a global project which will require a clear and transparent method for evaluating its success. The FDI will allow to estimate which NAs will be able to use the allocated funds with greater impact on the local football scene and help shape communities. The same logic can be applied to continental federations, which run their own development programs (e.g., UEFA actively promotes the Hat-Trick Programme).

4. *Distribution of voting and decision-making power*

Hamel (2009) states that "hierarchies need to be dynamic, so that power flows rapidly toward those who are adding value and away from those who aren't." It is a logical thought that those who prove to be better leaders and contribute more to corporate success should be granted more authority. However, FIFA adopts an approach where each member association has the same amount of decision-making power. The authors comprehend that FIFA's "one country—one vote" rule during the election procedures of the organization's president is dictated by the need to conform with the requirement of the Swiss civil code, which prohibits member discrimination. However the matter of selection of representatives in FIFA's governing committees could be reviewed as a possible platform where more "contributing" nations should be involved in the strategic decision-making.

5. *Intangible incentives*

Modern sport is based on incentives; however, due to its rapid commercialization, most incentives have become financially driven. A composite development index of a particular sport could provide its International Federation with the opportunity to implement an intangible motivation scheme, which would force member federations to strive toward greater feats. Similar to the practices of the FIFA/Coca-Cola Ranking, a merit system may be introduced, that is, "Best development program," "Most improved development efforts," etc.

NOTES

1. See http://www.doingbusiness.org/ for further details and data.
2. Win in 90 (or 120) minutes—3, win by penalty—2, draw in 90 (or 120) minutes or loss by penalties—1, losing 90 (or 120) minutes—0.
3. Friendly match—1, qualifying match of a continental or world championship—2.5, final stage of a continental championship and confederations cup—3, final stage of the FIFA World Cup—4.
4. A team's skill level is determined by its position in the FIFA Ranking. A country's rank is subtracted from 200. If a country holds the number 1 position in the ranking it receives 200. If a country is ranked 150 or lower—then it receives 50.
5. Depending on the confederation that a country is associated with it receives a continental coefficient. At this point confederation are given the following values: South America—1, Europe—0.99, North America, Africa, Asia and Oceania—0.85.
6. URL: http://www.fifa.com/mm/document/fifafacts/r&a-wwr/52/00/99/fs-590_06e_wwr-new.pdf
7. Relevant on March 2, 2017.

Chapter 3

Football Development Index

Dimensions and Indicators

This chapter will introduce the reader to the relevant scientific literature on potential dimensions and indicators of football development, how the indicator selection process was conducted, and how they were treated in order to ensure international comparability.

POTENTIAL DIMENSIONS AND INDICATORS

Literature on composite indicator design notes that the selection of factors plays a vital role in its methodological framework (Bandura, 2008; Freudenberg, 2003; Santos & Santos, 2014). The UNDP Human Development Report (UNDP, 2010) as well as Nardo et al. (2008) conclude that the factors included in a composite index should be:

a. Based on previous academic literature, confirming the presence of cause-effect relationships between dimension, factors, and indicators;
b. Covering a substantial (if not all) nations included in the index (in our case—more than 200).

Our literature review focuses on identifying the possible dimensions and factors of football development, which will be cross-referenced with the ability to obtain trustworthy and (preferably) publicly available data.

As already established, sporting performance, which from now on will be referred to in this book as "on-pitch performance," is an obvious dimension of the multidimensional concept of football development. It is obvious that this dimension will encompass elite sport results, since only at this level sporting results are regarded a no. 1 priority.

The FIFA/Coca-Cola Ranking is an official indicator for measuring the performance of a male national A-team. The FIFA Women's World Ranking estimates the results of the female national A-team. Surprisingly, no other official indicator is used by FIFA to assess the achievements of youth teams or teams of other varieties of football (i.e., beach soccer and futsal). Such an oversight by the football community is hard to objectify, since youth teams serve as a foundation to the future results at elite level (Martindale, Collins & Abraham, 2007; Darren & Geraldine, 2010).

The on-pitch performance of clubs is also an important aspect of a nation's overall sporting achievements. Solberg (2008) tested the impact of the *Bosman* ruling, which apart from its other implications abolished the practice of foreign player limitations within the EU. The study showed that the policy change allowed representatives of less "favorable" footballing nations to compete within the leading leagues of Europe, which also boosted the on-pitch results of their national teams. Club performance on a global scale should be measured through international competitions. As previously discussed, some continental federations calculate their own club rankings (i.e., UEFA—Europe; AFC—Asia; CAF—Africa). Due to the fact that calculation methodologies vary significantly, we propose to calculate results of all confederations in a unified manner using UEFA's scoring system (UEFA, 2017).

A clear concern is the possible correlation between the results of clubs and national teams at elite level. Although the statistical compatibility of the indicators will be addressed in the latter section of this book, it is important to have an understanding of the barriers lying ahead.

On-pitch performance is obviously an "end" of football development—something which shows the result, but not the manner in which it was achieved. The Football Development Index framework is aimed at not only comprehending where elite results are higher, but also determining what factors contribute to these ends. At this point it is important to establish the "means" for achieving these "ends."

De Bosscher, De Knop, Van Bottenburg, and Shibli (2006) proposed nine meso-level pillars for explaining international sporting success: financial support, structure, and organization of sport policies, sport participation, talent identification and development system, athletic and post career support, training facilities, coaching provision and development, participation in international competitions, and scientific research. The subsequent literature review will be focused on identifying the possible football-specific indicators that can be used to evaluate these factors.

The matter of financial support is most relevant to the global football scene. However, as it was already explicitly discussed in this book, FIFA uses a "one nation–one amount" approach in allocating development funding. Therefore, the only possible way to differentiate the financial support of football in each country is by evaluating the budget of their national FA's development programs and state-funded programs. However, it is a fair ex ante thought that this data will hardly be made public.

De Bosscher et al. (2009) propose a number of indicators to assess the structure and organization of sport policies, the majority of which are deemed to be subjective. Therefore, in our opinion, the inclusion of these factors would introduce unnecessary bias to the FDI framework, since it will be equally hard to collect and validate such information.

Sport participation is a vital part of sports development as was determined previously. Frick and Wicker (2015) were able to derive a statistically significant link between sporting success of the German national football team (male and female) and the increase in amateur sport participation (via number of club memberships, number of sports clubs and number of teams) within the country, which is known as the trickle-down effect. The most relevant increase in memberships in sports clubs (2.88%) was detected after the male national team won the World Cup. Additionally, the authors used a regression analysis to find that the year following Germany's World Cup victory the number of sports clubs increased by 1,397 and the number of teams—by 6,573. However, the authors were forced to conclude that female football success was mostly irrelevant in terms of affecting amateur sport participation.

Hanstad and Skille (2010) examined data of mass participation in biathlon activities in Norway and also attempted to determine a causal relationship between elite sport success and amateur sport population involvement. The findings of the research indicate the existence of an indirect relationship between Norway's biathlon national team achievements and mass sport participation. However, the authors state that biathlon might not be the best sport to determine such relationships, since it is clearly surpassed by football and skiing in the number of registered participants. The article also states that there is almost no link between mass sport participation and TV audience, since biathlon is the country's number one viewed sport, though there are merely 5,000 people involved in the sport. These findings of previous research projects point to the necessity of using the amount of registered football players and the amount of amateur football clubs as global football assessment criteria.

Recent papers have also proposed to use social media engagement as a determinant of interest in a particular phenomenon (Fischer & Reuber, 2011). With the amount of subscribers of several social media accounts of football federations, clubs and players now surpassing the 1 million mark, it is obvious that social media interaction should be regarded as a possible factor of football development. A clear debate would be how to properly assess this factor and what social media platforms are to be used. Various scientific contributions have suggested using absolute measures such as the total number of page and/or post "likes" (Gerlitz & Helmond, 2013) and page "followers" (Pérez, Bolívar & Hernández, 2012). Bonsón and Ratkai (2013) believe that the primary purpose of Facebook pages is to generate "engagement" within the news feed. Ángeles Oviedo-García et al. (2014) proposed several social media engagement metrics, such as the "ratio of interest," "ratio of effective interest," and "engagement of Facebook," which incorporate post likes, shares, comments, impressions, and reach. Miranda et al. (2014) proposed a composite indicator to assess the effectiveness of corporate Facebook pages, titled the "Facebook Assessment Index."

There is a sufficient literature base regarding the issue of infrastructural effects on sports participation. Hallmann, Wicker, Breuer, and Schönherr (2012) examined the relationship between several sport facility variables and participation among the population in sports which they are designed for. The findings of the research confirm the results of previous similar surveys: infrastructure development is an important determinant of overall sports development, since it has an influence on mass sport.

It is evident that insufficient sports infrastructure hampers sport development (Lim et al., 2011). Infrastructure benefits both amateur and elite sport, providing them with facilities for a better playing and training environment (Limstrand & Reher, 2008). Mass sport can survive purely on facility availability, since most amateur teams play for fun rather than for national pride and million dollar prizes.

Elite football, aside from training and competition facilities, also requires a structured talent development plan. It is impossible to achieve football supremacy in a day or even a year. On par with proper infrastructure development, football talent development needs qualified personnel which leads and monitors player progression (Cushion, 2010). Amorose (2007) states that coaches have a serious influence on player behavior, and athletic and technical abilities. The majority of the research regarding sport coaches mostly revolves around their effect on various athletic and nonathletic characteristics of players. The impact of coaching availability on elite sport performances is mostly neglected by the scientific society.

Apart from athletes and coaches there is a third component of any sporting spectacle—referees (McFee, 2004). A conducted literature review has helped the authors identify a clear research gap on the topic of referees having a direct impact on sports development. There are several notable works regarding psychological aspects of sport refereeing (Kaissidis-Rodafinos & Anshel, 2000; MacMahon, Helsen, Starkes & Weston, 2007; Mascarenhas, Collins, & Mortimer, 2005)—though none of them address the matter of referees having a direct impact on sports development.

Boeri and Severgnini (2012), while examining the main reasons for the downfall of Italian football, used match attendance and TV audience as the main indicators of the level of public interest toward football. Baranzini, Ramirez, and Weber (2008) used match attendance and match TV audience as proxies for measuring overall demand of football in Switzerland. Stadium attendance has been a well-discussed topic in the academic literature and has severely changed its conceptual foundations from being merely determined by the uncertainty of outcome of match and weather as was noted in the seminal paper of Neal (1964). Some academic scholars have even opted to review the determinants of both attendance and broadcasting data within a single paper (Buraimo, 2008; Buraimo & Simmons, 2009), which also reveals a potential overlap between the indicators.

Numerous recent contributions to the academic literature have revealed that attendance figures depend on proper hooliganism levels at matches (Andreff & Scelles, 2015; Scelles et al., 2016), competitive intensity (Scelles et al., 2013, 2016), adequate pricing (Pawlowski & Anders, 2012), proper scheduling (Buraimo, 2008), league market size (Buraimo & Simmons, 2009), as well as other factors. Therefore, including stadium attendance as an indicator of football development allows to latently incorporate various other features that serve as inputs for attracting fans to watch live games. The works of Buraimo and Simmons (2015) as well as Scelles (2017) point to the fact that most of gate attendance determinants overlap with the factors affecting TV-audience with the only exception being player quality represented through wages. It is our belief that ultimately the inclusion of any of the two indicators would be a good addition to the FDI; however, ex ante predictions point to data availability being a serious issue.

Due to the fact that the authors were unable to determine any other possible indicators to represent the factors proposed by De Bosscher, De Knop, Van Bottenburg, and Shibli (2006), a panel of experts specializing in football development was assembled in order to "fill the gaps." The expert panel comprised six representatives of the Football Union of Russia (Russian football's governing body), two of which were also members of UEFA committees. After a series of three meetings with detailed discussions the expert panel slightly modified the pillars proposed by De Bosscher, De Knop, Van Bottenburg, and Shibli (2006) as well as provided valuable insight on new potential indicators that could be introduced to the Football Development Index framework. The process of expert deliberation was conducted using a Delphi method, where each panel member prior to each meting received a questionnaire with all potential football development indicators. The experts then had a dichotomous choice between relevant and irrelevant. Each expert meeting then revolved around discussing the aggregated results of the survey. Experts were also allowed to introduce new potential factors, which were then included in the next questionnaires prior to the second and third meetings. The finalized list of potential factors and indicators, which includes the

Table 3.1 Potential Indicators of the Football Development Index

Potential Factors	Potential Indicators	Based On
Clubs	Club rankings	Authors and Expert Panel
National teams	FIFA/Coca-Cola Ranking	Lasek, Szlávik, and Bhulai (2013)
	FIFA World Women's Ranking	
	World Football Elo Ranking	
	Results of futsal national teams	Authors and Expert Panel
	Results of beach soccer national teams	
	Results of youth teams at FIFA World Cups	
Structure	No potential quantitative indicator	Authors and Expert Panel
Club performance	Continental club rankings	Authors and Expert Panel
Financial support	Budget of FA's development programs (strategy)	De Bosscher, De Knop, Van Bottenburg, and Shibli (2006) and Expert Panel
	State funding allocation to football development programs	Frick and Wicker (2015)
Amateur participation	Number of people involved in the sport	
	Number of amateur clubs	
	Number of amateur teams	
Athletic and post-career support	Violation of player contracts	Expert Panel
	Post-career coaching programs for players	Expert Panel
	Post-career learning programs for players (except for coaching)	Expert Panel
Interest in football	Match attendance	Baranzini, Ramirez, and Weber (2008); Boeri and Severgnini (2012); Andreff and Scelles (2015); Scelles (2017); Buraimo (2008); Buraimo and Simmons (2009)
	TV audience	
	Social media account followers	Pérez, Bolívar, and Hernández (2012). Bonsón and Ratkai (2013); Ángeles Oviedo-García et al. (2014); Cha et al. (2010)
	Social media account engagement	

Infrastructure	Facebook Assessment Index	Miranda et al. (2014)
	Training centers (academies)	Based on Hallmann, Wicker, Breuer, and Schönherr (2012)
	Football fields	
	Football-specific stadiums	
	Sports medicine centers	De Bosscher et al. (2009)
Personnel	Coaches	De Bosscher et al. (2009)
	Referees	Expert Panel
	Administrative staff	Expert Panel
	Development officers	Expert Panel
International competitions	Hosting international football tournaments	De Bosscher et al. (2009)
Talent identification	Number of national squads	Expert Panel
	Youth players	
Scientific research	Funding allocated to football-specific scientific research	De Bosscher et al. (2009) and Expert Panel
	Partner universities of the FA	
	Scientific breakthroughs implemented	

Source: Created by the authors

findings of the literature review and expert panel discussions, is presented in Table 3.1.

INDICATOR SPECIFICATION AND DATA AVAILABILITY

Nardo et al. (2008) recommend using only trustworthy sources with verifiable and relevant data. The Social Progress Index Methodological Report (Social Progress Imperative, 2016) underlines the importance for the data to be publicly available, which ensures transparency and independency from intentional overestimation. After due deliberation and research the initial list of potential indicators was limited to 12 indicators and, in line with the recommendations of the expert panel, grouped into three dimensions: on-pitch performance, popularity, and environment. This logic is somewhat in line with the conclusions of previous studies (Bayle and Madella, 2002; Madella et al., 2005; Papadimitrou & Taylor, 2000; Winand et al., 2011) that emphasize the three strategic goals of national sports organizations: elite sports, sport for all, and customers.

The popularity dimension will encompass both amateur football represented though participation and club registration rates, as was used by Frick and Wicker (2015), as well as elite football represented through average match attendance of top-tier division. The environment dimension will include five indicators: youth (under-18) players, average stadium capacity, number of coaches, FIFA-licensed referees, and number of international squads. A clear concern would be the possible overlap of the stadium capacity and match attendance indicators, since there is a possible cause-effect relationship between the two. However, the later indicator encompasses only elite-level football, while the former is a necessary attribute of both amateur and elite level. Stadium capacity includes all football-specific stadiums currently active within a country, so countries such as the United States won't get an unfair advantage for having 100 thousand arenas, on which an association football match is played once or twice a year. This indicator is used as a proxy for overall football infrastructure, since it was the only indicator of this sort, on which valid data could be collected. The possibility of overlapping data is also minimized by the fact that these indicators will be scaled. However, the introduction of such indicator has its fair amount of limitations. The most obvious of which is the white elephant problem, where big stadia are left almost without any sports-related action, because it is not economically viable to host regular matches there that won't fill the arena. We refer the reader to the contributions of Alm, Solberg, Storm, and Jakobsen (2016) for gaining a better understanding regarding this issue.

Table 3.2 Finalized List of FDI Indicators

Dimension	Indicator	Coding	Averaged by	Scope	Source
On-pitch performance	Performance of national teams (beach, futsal and youth)	O1	Not averaged	2000–2014	FIFA and calculations of the authors
	FIFA Club rankings	O2		2014	FIFA
	FIFA Women's world ranking	O3		2014	UEFA, CAF, CONMEBOL, CONCACAF, AFC, OFC, and calculations of the authors
	FIFA/Coca-Cola Ranking	O4		2010–2014	FIFA
Popularity	Percentage of population playing football	P1	Population	2006	FIFA Big count, World Bank
	Number of amateur clubs divided by population	P2		2006	FIFA Big count, World Bank
	Average match attendance of top-division club	P3		2014	European-football-statistics.co.uk/, worldfootball.net
Environment	Percentage of youth (U-18) players out of all footballers	E1	Number of players	2006	FIFA Big count
	Average football stadium capacity	E2		2014	Worldstadiums.com
	Number of coaches divided by the number of all footballers	E3		2006	FIFA Big count
	Number of international FIFA-licensed referees	E4	Not averaged	2014	FIFA
	Number of international squads	E5		2014	Websites of NA's

The introduction of an appropriate scaling system is needed to make the inter-country comparisons relevant and valid. Nardo et al. (2008) recommend introducing ratio scale for each indicator to make the composite index invariant to changes in measurement units. Per capita adjustment is commonly used in order to "level the playing field" in cross-analyzing significantly varying objects. An additional meeting of the expert panel was called to decide the most appropriate adjustment technique.

All "Popularity" indicators will be averaged by a nation's overall population. This is explained by the essence of the concept of "popularity," which, according to the *Merriam-Webster Dictionary* (2017), is defined as "something suitable for the majority; commonly liked or approved; relating to the general public." The rationale for averaging attendance figures is explained by the fact that population is included as control variable within most fan demand studies (Andreff & Scelles, 2015; Scelles, 2017; Buraimo, 2008; Buraimo & Simmons, 2009). However, it is also fair to assume that stadium attendance is constrained by stadium capacity, since you cannot sell more tickets to a single game than the available amount of seats. Therefore, an alternative to averaging the indicator by population would be to incorporate a stadium capacity utilization measure that would show the average percentage of seats sold out during football matches. However, this indicator has significant limitations as well, since it does not standardize the marginal effect from the increase of the number of fans attending live games. With this logic in mind we selected to standardize attendance figure using population rates.

Three (E1-E3) "environment" indicators will be averaged using the overall number of football players within a country. Table 3.2 shows the finalized list of FDI indicators.

Similar to the Human Development Index we propose to use a triad of marking groups to form the Football Development Index. These groups will incorporate the above selected variables. All of this will lead to the construction of conventional tool, which will allow to accurately characterize football development and assess the game's growing potential. The marking groups were structured accordingly:

1. On-pitch performance.
2. Football popularity.
3. Football development environment.

Chapter 4

Calculation Model

DATA ANALYSIS

It is essential for the data to be normally distributed to account for the results being adequately reflected in the final index. The only indicator showing normal distribution is the number of referees (Table 4.1). The other indicators show high degrees of skewness, which means this data has to be transformed. Nardo et al. (2008) propose to use logarithmic transformation, similar to what is done to GNI per capita in the Human Development Index framework (UNDP, 2010). This type of transformation accounts for the difference in increase of a one-unit measure for a lower level of performance compared to the identical improvement for a high level performance.

The components of a composite index have to be statistically compatible (Nardo et al., 2008). The most widely applied method is the Cronbach coefficient alpha (C-alpha), which was introduced by Cronbach (1951). The C-alpha is used to test the consistency of the value throughout the selected dataset using their paired calculation levels. C-alpha equaling zero means that the indicators are not at all correlated and thus the data cannot be incorporated into an additive model, while C-alpha equaling one means that the indicators are perfectly correlated.

$$a_c = \left(\frac{Q}{Q-1}\right)\frac{\sum_{i \neq j} \text{cov}(x_i x_j)}{\text{var}(x_o)} = \left(\frac{Q}{Q-1}\right)\left(1 - \frac{\sum_j \text{var}(x_j)}{\text{var}(x_o)}\right); c = 1, \ldots, M; i, j = 1, \ldots, Q \quad (4.1)$$

where M—the number of variables (in our case, countries) considered;
Q—the number of indicators tested.

Table 4.2 demonstrates the values of the Cronbach's alpha for each of the three dimensions. All dimensions show high compatibility with values being

Table 4.1 Distribution of FDI Data

Indicators	Skewness	Std. err. of Skewness	Number of Observations
Performance of national teams (beach, futsal and youth)	3.911		
FIFA/Coca-Cola Ranking;	1.288		
Club rankings	2.255		
FIFA World Women's Ranking	1.210		
Percentage of population playing football	4.041		
Number of amateur clubs divided by population	3.324		
Average match attendance of top-division club	3.265	0.168	185
Percentage of youth (U-18) players out of all footballers	1.059		
Average football stadium capacity	4.823		
Number of coaches divided by the number of all footballers	5.988		
Number of international FIFA-licensed referees	0.318		
Number of international squads	0.695		

Source: created by the authors.

Table 4.2 Cronbach's Alpha Values for the FDI Dimensions

Dimension	Number of Indicators	Cronbach's Alpha
On-pitch performance	4	0.825
Popularity	3	0.743
Environment	5	0.644

Source: created by the authors.

higher than the acceptable cutoff point of 0.6 (Loewenthal, 2001). The overall Cronbach's alpha calculated with all 12 indicators equals 0.812, which confirms the appropriateness of compiling the dimensions into a composite index.

DATA NORMALIZATION

Data normalization is an essential part of designing a composite index, since it brings the measurement scale to unified manner throughout the whole dataset, making it validly comparable. Nardo et al. (2008) highlight a number of normalization techniques: z-score, mini-max, ranking, distance to a reference, above-or-below-mean. It is crucial that the normalized data should be: (a) easily interpretable for both policy-makers and the general public; (b) capturing not only the difference between the scores of each variable but also the degree of difference. The most suitable techniques look to be the z-score and mini-max methods.

Z-scores allow to standardize each observation as well as the degree of differences between each individual factor. The Z-score for each criterion can be calculated using the following formula:

$$Z_{ij} = \frac{x_{ij} - \overline{X_j}}{S_j} \qquad (4.2)$$

Where i—an indication of each criterion;
j—an indication of each country;
X_{ij}—the value of an i-country for its j-criterion;
$\overline{X_j}$—the mean value for the j-criterion;
S_j—the standard deviation of the j-criterion.

Z-scores derive both positive and negative values based on whether the country's score is above or below the mean value of the selected criterion. This calculation peculiarity allows differentiating countries into above and below average performers. Thus, we derive a benchmarking tool that easily points out the best applied practices. Another advantage of the Z-score method is that it allows assessing the best practices not merely on a global scale (i.e., among all 209 members), but also based on various factors: geography, population, climate, socioeconomic development, etc. Therefore, it will be possible to not only benchmark the best global practices, but also lower the benchmarking continental scale, or assess the best football development approaches among countries with severe weather conditions or low GDP rates. The Z-scoring can be used to monitor the average football development level (on both global and continental scales) as well as differentiate nations as above and below average performers.

The min-max method normalizes values on a scale from 0 to 1 using the following equation:

$$x'_{ij} = \frac{x_{ij} - \min(X_j)}{\max(X_j) - \min(X_j)} \qquad (4.3)$$

where x_i is the value an i-nation within a j-indicator;
$\max X_j$ is the maximum value within the j-indicator;
$\min X_j$ is the minimum value within the j-indicator.

WEIGHTING

Every composite indicator comprises several dimensions each one of which contributes in its own manner to the overall outcome. More commonly, some factors can produce a larger impact on the final result than others. However, the degree of this impact and the exact difference in significance between the factors cannot always be adequately determined and objectified without employing specially designed techniques.

The most relevant classification on weighting approaches can be found in the excellent paper of Decancq and Lugo (2013), where the authors proposed three groups of weights: normative, data-driven, and hybrid. Normative methods are based on the notion that the importance of a single factor can be explained by normative logic and experience. Data-driven methods propose using statistical and econometric modeling to establish the quantitative representation of the trade-offs between the dimensions based on previous data. Hybrid methods propose to incorporate both normative and data-driven methods in order to explain the setting of weights. Hybrid weights are not developed within this book.

Normative Weights

Decancq and Lugo (2013) highlight three normative weighting approaches: equal/arbitrary, price-based, and expert opinion. Obviously, in these methods the values of the weights are normatively inspired; however, there are few (debatable) ways of objectifying the reasonable trade-offs between the dimensions, derived from normative logic (Fleurbaey, 2008).

As noted by Decancq and Lugo (2013) equal weights (EW) are most commonly applied in multidimensional indices. Among the main merits of the method, the authors highlight its simplicity and the ability to assign even importance to the factors, in cases where it is hard to clearly grade the factors by the means of their contribution to the end-result. Among the more renowned index systems using equal weighting Böhringer and Jochem (2007) acknowledge the Human Development Index, Ecological Footprint Index, Living Planet Index, Index of Sustainable Economic Welfare, and others. The wide application of equal weighting can also be explained by the fact that they make these models easier to interpret for the public and policy-makers.

However, it is a fairly justified statement that the equal weighting method is far from being undisputable, as mentioned in the work of Chowdhury and Squire (2006). Belhadj (2012) goes further by rightfully stating that the substitutability of the factors included in the model and the trade-offs between the dimensions should be made explicit, while equal weights certainly denote the possibility of doing so. The equal weights method was also criticized in the work of Ravallion (1997) in the framework of the Human Development Index. Most notably, the authors contemplate that, contrary to common belief, an extra year of life can be measured in monetary value and the differentiation of the "cost" of an extra year of life between poor and rich countries is remarkably high. A more recent paper criticizing the methodology of the Human Development Index by Palazzi and Lauri (2013) furthered the rationale of Ravallion (1997). The authors provide an empirical solution of the equal weighting problem by conducting a statistical analysis for the purpose of determining whether or not there is a relation between the three components, which would help objectifying the importance of each dimension.

Santeramo (2015) argues that equal weights may induce double counting in hierarchical indexes where subgroups have a varying amount of factors. Subsequently, since every factor will be assigned equal importance, the subgroup comprising most factors will have the biggest contribution to the value of the composite index. Such a comment is most relevant for the Football Development Index, since it has a two-level hierarchy index, where the three dimensions comprise a varying number of indicators. More precisely, the "Football Environment" dimension contains five indicators, while "On-pitch Performance" has only four indicators and "Football Popularity" only three indicators. This particular issue is the main drawback of the FDI structure that forces the authors to review the possibility of incorporating more sophisticated weighting approaches in order to ensure the robust nature of the index. However, an equal weighting approach to determining the trade-offs between the three key dimensions seems to be the most reasonable alternative, since they represent the cornerstone of this research.

Expert Opinion Weights

Expert opinion modeling implies adopting the conclusions of specifically designed expert panels to account for the weights of each dimension. The expert method can be adopted in those cases where the assessed phenomenon does not have a clear quantitative representation. There are two typical methods to elicit views from experts: Budget Allocation Process and Analytic Hierarchy Process (Decancq & Lugo, 2013).

The Budget Allocation Process (BAP) method implies providing the chosen panel of experts with a certain amount of contingent points that have to be distributed among the dimensions of the model. The final weights of each factor are derived as the mean of all points allocated by the experts. The common practice proposes the allocation of 100 points for simplifying calculations (Nardo et al., 2008).

The notable merits of the method include transparency and simplicity. The main setback of all expert opinion methods is their subjective nature, since the selected experts might be driven by personal interests rather than experience and logic. There are ways to minimize these risks. Nardo et al. (2008) recommend to compile the expert panel with representatives from various professional fields and exclude the possibility of all specialists being focused on an individual dimension. Stratification is one of the solutions to this problem, so that the sample of experts represents the general set of variables, which will be included in the model. In this case, if we intend to construct an index-based assessment tool for all FIFA member nations then each FA should be presented in the expert panel. If the finalized set of weights causes debate among the expert panel then consequent revaluation and iteration may be conducted until a compromise is achieved.

The concept of Analytical hierarchy process (AHP) was introduced by Saaty (1988) and originated from multi-attribute decision-making. Any problem may be decomposed into a certain structure comprising both quantitative and qualitative aspects. Expert opinions are extracted by using a pairwise comparison between each of the dimensions (Nardo et al., 2008). Contrary to the Budget Allocation Approach, the AHP enables decision-makers to derive weights as opposed to arbitrarily assigning them.

Saaty (1998) justifies the approach of the AHP by stating that the refinements of mathematical trade-offs cannot always provide valid conclusions, since some problems possess complex subjective qualities. The AHP is intended to solve dilemmas invariant to politics and behavior. This is achieved by proper scaling: "what sort of numbers to use, and how to correctly combine the priorities resulting from them." The measurement is based on the willingness to forego a given variable in exchange for another. The relative weights of the individual indicators are calculated using an eigenvector. This method makes it possible to check the consistency of the comparison matrix through the calculation of the eigenvalues (Nardo et al., 2008).

The AHP has been applied in a wide range of research fields to establish weights during multi-criteria decision-making. Babic and Plazibat (1998) used the Analytical hierarchy process to determine the importance of business efficiency indicators in order to construct a ranking of enterprises. Labib, Williams, and O'Connor (1998) applied the AHP in order to prioritize machines and their faults based on different criteria. This was used for the purpose of obtaining criticality output, so that an optimal maintenance system for the machines can be derived. The research introduced a six level hierarchy formulation of AHP. The first level is criteria assessment, and the second level is supposed to identify the most crucial of the machines. In the third level the failure categories are grouped into the general ones. This helps the decision-makers to identify areas where different maintenance skills are essential. The fourth level is concerned with the specific faults related to each fault categories. The final two levels are related to the detail failure component of the major sections.

Chowdhury and Squire (2006) conducted a survey using the expert of opinions of development researchers throughout the world to reevaluate the weights of the Human Development Index (which uses equal weights). The findings of the paper showcased that contrary to major criticism of the equal weighting adopted by the HDI, the Budget Allocation Process provided results that granted almost the same significance to all three dimensions.

Tomao et al. (2015) applied Principal Component Analysis (PCA), equal weights, and BAP approaches to identify the significance of the factors included in a tree risk assessment model. The subsequent cross-comparison of the weights using the derived methods showcased highly similar results. The linear correlation coefficient was higher than 0.90 in all cases and statistically significant at a 1% level (Figure 4.1). Based on these calculations, the authors state that the weighting method did not substantially affect the results of their assessment. However, this is not an axiomatic deliberation; therefore, results may vary based on the data.

Table 4.3 presents the results of the weight values for each indicator calculated with three different methods. The weights of indicators within each dimension equal 1, since each dimension is allocated an equal 0.33 weight in the composite index. As we can see, the values vary significantly, with the only significant ($p < 0.01$) correlation found between EW and PCA weights of 0.794, which can be regarded as surprising, since the former is known to be the simplest weighting method, while the later method is often labeled as one of the more complex approaches.

Although the weight values presented in Table 4.3 vary significantly, the overall index is not significantly affected by the changes in the selection of the weighting method, with all three calculations having statistically significant ($p < 0.01$) correlations of 0.980 and higher (Figure 4.1).

Given that it is clear that a selection of a more straightforward weighting method does not scrutinize the calculations, the adoption of equal weights

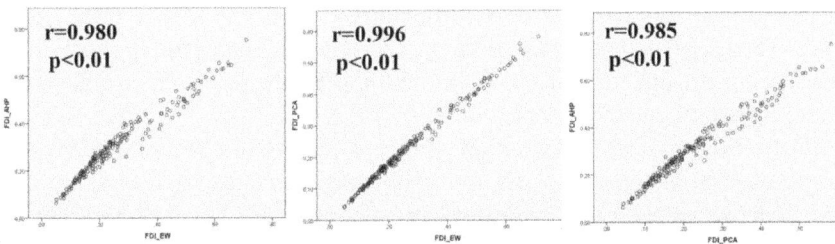

Figure 4.1 Scatterplots of the Football Development Index Calculated with Three Different Weighting Methods. Created by the authors.

Table 4.3 Weight Values of FDI Indicators Calculated with Three Different Methods

Dimensions	Indicators	Weighting Method*		
		EW	AHP	PCA
On-pitch performance	O1	25%	11,73%	21,23%
	O2	25%	25,28%	27,24%
	O3	25%	11,09%	24,25%
	O4	25%	51,91%	27,28%
Popularity	P1	33%	53,96%	25,54%
	P2	33%	16,34%	37,12%
	P3	33%	29,70%	37,34%
Environment	E1	20%	42,30%	13,77%
	E2	20%	9,11%	22,14%
	E3	20%	26,69%	15,50%
	E4	20%	14,14%	25,40%
	E5	20%	7,76%	23,19%

Source: created by the authors.
* The weight values equal 1 within each dimension.

seems appropriate to make the Football Development Index easier to interpret for policy-makers.

AGGREGATION

The two main aggregation techniques commonly used in designing composite indexes are linear and geometric methods. As stated by Nardo et al. (2008), the selection of the aggregation method is dictated by the existence of interdependence between the variables. Linear aggregation is applicable in frameworks where the factors' marginal contribution can be assessed separately. This logic makes linear aggregation inapplicable to aggregating the values of each dimension, since one indicator cannot be used as a substitute for the other. However, geometric aggregation is inapplicable if values are equal or below zero, which will be obviously the case for countries that do not have an active female national team and, subsequently, have 0 in female FIFA rankings. The use of geometric aggregation, therefore, excludes the application of z-scores, since this normalization method implies the calculation of negative values when below the mean.

With this logic in mind we propose to use linear aggregation to derive the score of each dimension, since in a unidimensional capacity it is likely that a low performance in one indicator can be compensated by a better value of same-dimension indicator (e.g., better performance of a beach soccer team can compensate the poor results of the nation's futsal team):

$$Dimension_j = \sum_{q=1}^{Q} w_q I_{jq}; \; w_q = 1/Q, \sum w_q = 1, \tag{4.4}$$

W_q—the weight of a q indicator;
I_{jq}—the normalized value of a j-country for its q-indicator.

The geometric aggregation method will be used to calculate the composite index via the linearly aggregated values of each dimension:

$$FDI_j = \prod_{q=1}^{Q=3} Dimension_{jq}^{(\frac{1}{3})}; Dimension_{jq} \geq 0, \tag{4.5}$$

Geometric aggregation seems to be the more appropriate fit for the final calculation stage. This is explained by the fact that in cases, where a nation scores high on one of the dimensions, but performs way below on other sub-dimensions, it would not have the chance to receive a high aggregate index value. For example, nation A scores 6 on on-pitch performance and 1 on both popularity and environment, thus resulting in a linearly aggregated index of 8 and a geometrically aggregated index of 1.82. But if nation B scores 2 on on-pitch performance and 3 on the other sub-dimensions, than it would also receive a linear aggregated score on 8, but its geometrically aggregated value would equal 2.62. The geometrically aggregated values seem to produce more adequate results, since they allow to account for the variance in all sub-dimensions.

Given that geometric aggregation only works well when all values are 0 or above, it would be more appropriate to incorporate the min-max normalization method instead of z-scores. The negative values produced by z-score normalization can scrutinize the aggregation process, since the negative value within a single indicator could lead to an overall negative value.

GROUPING

For the purpose of forming a more complete image of the overall ranking and a more descriptive interpretation of its results a 5-star grouping system was introduced (Pang & Lee, 2005): "5 stars"—very high, "1 star"—very low level of football development. The groups were formed in accordance with the results from all 12 criteria. According to the selected aggregation method the maximum value of national FDI would equal 1, while the minimum would equal 0. In this case, nations will be allocated a particular football development level through five quintiles, each ranging within a 0.2 margin (Table 4.4).

Table 4.4 FDI Quintile Description

FDI quintile	FDI value	Interpretation
5 stars	From 0.8 to 1	Very high level of football development
4 stars	From 0.799 to 0.6	High level of football development
3 stars	From 0.599 to 0.4	Average level of football development
2 stars	From 0.399 to 0.2	Low level of football development
1 star	From 0.199 to 0	Very low level of football development

Source: Created by the authors.

The Kohonen self-organizing map (SOM) can be used as a clustering approach. The method was first introduced by Kohonen (1982) and allows to present multidimensional data (in our case—a 12-dimensional dataset) in a two-dimensional space. The clustering is performed by classifying nations with similar indicator vectors (the least distance between the variables). The SOM allows highlighting the nations with similar football development attributes: strong and weak aspects, roughly same FDI levels as well as similar development needs. This clustering method helps nations identify the most adjacent "neighbors" in terms of football development, which means that these nations will be the most suitable development practices for benchmarking purposes.

BENCHMARKING

The benchmarking procedure of football development practices will be based on: (a) geographical and (b) economic attributes. Countries grouped in the highest quintile within their confederation will be labeled as a "continental football development benchmark." Benchmarking via economic attributes will be a more complex procedure, embodying the approach used in the Social Progress Index (Social Progress Imperative, 2016). Cumulative GDP (PPP) will be used as a proxy for economic development, similar to what was done by Kuper and Szymanski (2010). Countries will be compiled into peer groups of 15, so that the degree of difference in GDP values remains semi-controlled. The median FDI value for each peer group will be calculated (the use of the median instead of the mean is explained by the need to control for outliers). Countries with the highest FDI value within each peer group will be named football development benchmarks, while the nations with the lowest FDI values will be known as underperformers within their corresponding peer group.

Chapter 5

Football Development Report 2013[1]

This chapter will provide the reader with the results of the first calculation of the FDI on a global scale with a detailed breakdown of the findings within each confederation. Based on the adopted benchmarking procedure the best and worst practices of football development will be discussed as well.

GLOBAL FOOTBALL DEVELOPMENT SCENE

Table 5.1 shows the results of the calculations for the first dimension of the Football Development Index, which is on-pitch performance. As we can see, Brazil and Germany have an advantage compared to the other nations. Brazil's top spot can be explained by their excellent results not only on the "big pitch" of 11 on 11 football, but also their dominance in beach soccer and futsal, which are the areas where German football still lacks quality. Obviously, Germany's talent development program introduced in 2002 has served as catalyst for lifting the nation's football results to an unprecedented level.

The top 20 of the "on-pitch performance" dimension is dominated by UEFA (Europe) and CONMEBOL (South America) representatives, while CONCACAF (North America) and AFC (Asia) were able to contribute only two representatives each.

The second dimension "popularity" saw the Republic of Ireland take top spot, indisputably dominating significantly with the help of the "registered clubs" indicator (Table 5.2). Ireland's grassroots sports development system has always been seen as one of the more successful mainly due to the efforts of the Gaelic Athletics Association (GAA); see Gallagher, O'Connor and Gilmore (2016) for more details. However, more recent years have proved to be very productive for the Football Association of Ireland (FAI) as well and

Table 5.1 The Top 20 Nations Based on the "On-Pitch Performance" Dimension

Nation	National Teams	Club Results	FIFA Female Ranking	FIFA Male Ranking	On-pitch Performance	Rank
Brazil	1.00	0.78	0.90	0.76	0.861	1
Germany	0.61	0.82	1.00	1.00	0.859	2
Spain	0.60	1.00	0.86	0.66	0.779	3
Argentina	0.58	0.61	0.74	0.89	0.707	4
France	0.42	0.55	0.96	0.67	0.650	5
England	0.22	0.85	0.91	0.60	0.644	6
Italy	0.39	0.67	0.86	0.64	0.641	7
Netherlands	0.24	0.43	0.89	0.80	0.588	8
Portugal	0.30	0.65	0.71	0.67	0.584	9
Colombia	0.19	0.49	0.78	0.84	0.575	10
United States	0.51	0.21	0.99	0.48	0.548	11
Mexico	0.36	0.44	0.80	0.53	0.532	12
Belgium	0.08	0.38	0.79	0.82	0.517	13
Chile	0.14	0.57	0.72	0.59	0.505	14
Russia	0.17	0.52	0.82	0.45	0.492	15
Switzerland	0.13	0.37	0.84	0.63	0.491	16
Japan	0.41	0.26	0.96	0.32	0.488	17
Ukraine	0.12	0.45	0.81	0.49	0.468	18
South Korea	0.28	0.38	0.84	0.27	0.444	19
Czech Republic	0.12	0.31	0.76	0.57	0.442	20

Source: Created by the authors based on AFC (2017); FIFA (2015); Global Football Ranks (2017); UEFA (2017).

we can clearly see the positive results of the football development initiatives within the Republic of Ireland.

Germany had the highest absolute value of people participating in football activities—more than 6 million inhabitants playing football on a regular basis.

A somewhat surprising outcome is the presence of the Faroe Islands in the third spot. However, the review of empirical evidence shatters any sort of skepticism. With a population of roughly 31,000 people the nation has 8,094 people participating in football-related activities. The "popularity" dimensions produced more, let's say, "exotic" outcomes with countries such as Vanuatu and Namibia being put at the same level as renowned powerhouses such as England. Some findings might strike the general public as being even more surprising and difficult to comprehend. For instance, India and China are not usually perceived as the most frenzy football supporters, yet the figures of their average top tier football leagues attendance are the 4th (25 371 spectators) and 8th (18 740) best in the world, respectively. However, this fact also shads further light on the issue of population affecting stadium attendance.

Table 5.2 The Top 20 Nations Based on the "Popularity" Dimension

Country	Participation	Registered Clubs	Match Attendance	Popularity	Rank
Republic of Ireland	0.64	0.92	0.41	*0.656*	*1*
Germany	0.90	0.89	0.18	*0.655*	*2*
Faroe Islands	0.60	0.42	0.94	*0.653*	*3*
Scotland	0.61	0.93	0.40	*0.647*	*4*
Norway	0.68	0.83	0.40	*0.634*	*5*
Chile	0.79	0.82	0.29	*0.634*	*6*
Vanuatu	0.55	0.63	0.71	*0.633*	*7*
England	0.69	1.00	0.21	*0.633*	*8*
Sweden	0.70	0.82	0.35	*0.621*	*9*
Barbados	0.62	0.53	0.70	*0.616*	*10*
Slovakia	0.70	0.74	0.40	*0.613*	*11*
Czech Republic	0.69	0.81	0.34	*0.612*	*12*
Namibia	1.00	0.36	0.47	*0.611*	*13*
Denmark	0.65	0.78	0.39	*0.605*	*14*
Austria	0.71	0.74	0.36	*0.604*	*15*
Netherlands	0.71	0.80	0.30	*0.603*	*16*
Greece	0.61	0.85	0.33	*0.598*	*17*
New Zealand	0.86	0.51	0.41	*0.595*	*18*
Croatia	0.62	0.73	0.42	*0.588*	*19*
Iceland	0.54	0.53	0.69	*0.588*	*20*

Source: Created by the authors based on FIFA (2006); European-football-statistics.co.uk (2015); Worldfootball.net (2017).

It is also important to note that unlike in the "on-pitch performance" dimension not a single nation was able to score within the 5th quintile, meaning that no country has a "very high" level of football popularity.

The third and final dimension—"environment"—sees Belgium and the Republic of Ireland again taking the two top spots with England slightly behind in third (Table 5.3). Belgium's dominance is hardly a surprise given their "golden" generation of football players coming to prominence just now. It is interesting to see Qatar, the host of the upcoming 2022 FIFA World Cup, in 15th place with very high results within the "youth players," "stadium capacity," and "coaches" indicators.

The results of the Football Development Index are given in Table 5.4. They provide a differing perspective of the global football scene, which has been previously explained predominantly by the results of the male national A-team via the FIFA/Coca-Cola ranking. To verify this statement we tested the correlation links between the FDI dimensions and the FIFA/Coca-Cola ranking (Table 5.5).

Figure 5.1 presents the scatterplot of FDI and FIFA/Coca-Cola ranking values. The width of the plots representing each country are indicated by a

Table 5.3 The Top 20 Nations Based on the "Environment" Dimension

Country	Youth Players	Stadium Capacity	Coaches	FIFA Referees	Number of National Squads	Environment	Rank
Belgium	0.96	0.53	0.41	0.78	0.74	0.680	1
Republic of Ireland	0.97	0.48	0.49	0.43	1.00	0.671	2
England	0.90	0.50	0.59	0.63	0.74	0.670	3
France	0.93	0.46	0.31	0.85	0.79	0.668	4
Portugal	0.79	0.63	0.30	0.75	0.84	0.663	5
Netherlands	1.00	0.44	0.34	0.75	0.79	0.662	6
Poland	0.87	0.50	0.31	0.75	0.84	0.655	7
Italy	0.83	0.48	0.42	0.90	0.63	0.652	8
Uruguay	0.70	0.66	0.51	0.75	0.58	0.640	9
Sweden	0.96	0.49	0.37	0.65	0.74	0.640	10
Germany	0.93	0.43	0.32	0.78	0.74	0.639	11
Finland	0.89	0.48	0.44	0.58	0.74	0.624	12
Slovakia	1.00	0.42	0.38	0.63	0.68	0.622	13
Scotland	0.80	0.58	0.43	0.50	0.79	0.622	14
Qatar	0.80	0.90	0.75	0.33	0.32	0.619	15
Switzerland	0.89	0.54	0.35	0.63	0.68	0.618	16
Argentina	0.70	0.54	0.31	0.90	0.63	0.616	17
Denmark	0.97	0.55	0.43	0.50	0.63	0.615	18
Austria	0.98	0.47	0.47	0.60	0.53	0.608	19
Spain	0.81	0.53	0.32	0.90	0.47	0.608	20

Source: created by the authors based on FIFA (2006, 2015); Worldstadiums.com (2017).

Table 5.4 The Top 20 Nations Based on the Football Development Index

Nation	On-pitch Performance	Popularity	Environment	Football Development Index	Rank
Germany	0.859	0.655	0.639	0.711	1
Brazil	0.861	0.555	0.601	0.660	2
Spain	0.779	0.584	0.608	0.652	3
England	0.644	0.633	0.670	0.649	4
France	0.650	0.581	0.668	0.632	5
Italy	0.641	0.585	0.652	0.625	6
Netherlands	0.588	0.603	0.662	0.617	7
Argentina	0.707	0.517	0.616	0.609	8
Portugal	0.584	0.545	0.663	0.595	9
Belgium	0.517	0.554	0.680	0.580	10
Chile	0.505	0.634	0.575	0.569	11
Switzerland	0.491	0.557	0.618	0.553	12
Sweden	0.409	0.621	0.640	0.546	13
Czech Republic	0.442	0.612	0.592	0.543	14
United States	0.548	0.506	0.567	0.540	15
Denmark	0.396	0.605	0.615	0.528	16
Austria	0.397	0.604	0.608	0.526	17
Russia	0.492	0.506	0.581	0.525	18
Scotland	0.359	0.647	0.622	0.525	19
Colombia	0.575	0.506	0.477	0.518	20

Source: Created by the authors.

Table 5.5 Correlation Matrix of FDI Dimensions and FIFA/Coca-Cola Ranking

	On-pitch Performance	Popularity	Environment	FIFA/Coca-Cola Ranking	FDI
On-pitch performance	1				
Popularity	.463*	1			
Environment	.682*	.539*	1		
FIFA/Coca-Cola ranking	.849*	.451*	.648*	1	
FDI	.949*	.593*	.793*	.875*	1

Source: Created by the authors.
*p < 0.01.

country's FDI value. The scatterplot does not give much cause for speculation of a direct relationship between the two indicators; however, the possibility of clusters that can be formed within FDI framework should certainly be further assessed.

The visualization of the results is also an essential part of calculating international indexes and rankings, since it makes the outcomes easier to interpret for both policy-makers and the general public (Trame & Keßler, 2011).

52   Chapter 5

Figure 5.1 Two-Dimensional Scatterplot of FDI and FIFA/Coca-Cola Ranking Values. Created by the authors and IntellSoft Business Group.

Choropleth maps are the most popular visualization method for presenting data with geographic attributes (Crampton, 2004). Harrower and Brewer (2003) recommend using a green-red coloring scheme in order to ensure better contrast between the values of each nation. A 5-tone coloring scheme was introduced with each tone corresponding to a specific FDI quintile group: dark green for very high values, light green—high values, yellow—average values, orange—low values, red—very low values (Figure 5.2).

Mosaics are also a popular and informative way of presenting multidimensional data. A visualization mosaic is a composite graph comprising multiple visual representations juxtaposed in the same space, with each representation presenting a subset of a master dataset.

Figure 5.3 presents the visualization mosaic of the Football Development Index, its dimensions, and its indicators. The coloring scheme is identical to the one used in Figure 5.2. The rows of the mosaic represent the FDI indicators and dimensions, while the columns represent the nations, which sorted by the FDI ranks. As we can see, the largest downfall can be seen within the on-pitch performance dimension with the dominance of red-colored blocks being easily spotted in the upper-right corner of the mosaic. However, the popularity and environment dimensions show a more or less even distribution of values. These findings confirm to some extent the preliminary expectations that sporting results are not the sole determinant of football development. "The number of national squads" indicator seems to show a similar trend with on-pitch performance indicators, which can indicate the presence of a cause-effect relationship. Such a conclusion seems significantly feasible, since some nations are still unable to host not only beach soccer or futsal teams, but do not even have a single point within the Women's FIFA Rankings, since their female national teams do not participate in competitive matches.

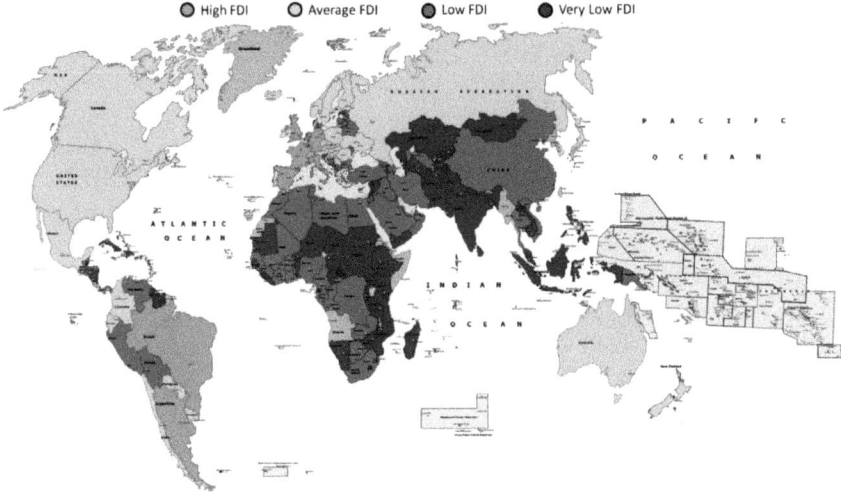

Figure 5.2 Global Choropleth Map Based on FDI Values. Created by the authors and IntellSoft Business Group

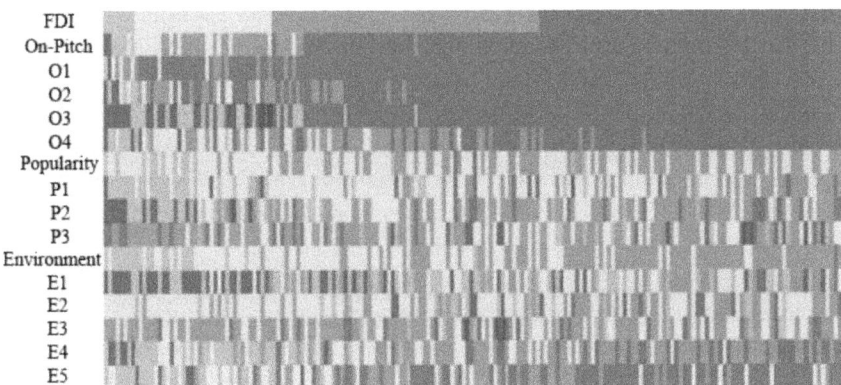

Figure 5.3 Visualization Mosaic of FDI Values. Created by the authors and IntellSoft Business Group.

The mosaic also allows us to see that not a single nation was able to receive a very high value (0.8 and higher—dark green coloring) in both the popularity and environment dimensions. Average match attendance of FDI leaders is actually showing an opposite trend with their values within other indicators. This can be largely explained by the fact that attendance figures were averaged by their population values, so the less populated nations scored better on this indicator. Apparently, even logarithmic transformation did not help to control for this issue, which could also mean that the more populated are still not using their full potential of attracting spectators to football matches.

CONTINENTAL FOOTBALL DEVELOPMENT SCENE

The continental choropleth maps based on FDI values are presented in Figures 5.4–5.9.

The African (CAF) and Asian (AFC) continents seem to present a dominating presence of low and very low football development levels, which should be noted as a real concern for their continental federations and to FIFA.

BEST PRACTICES

The distribution of nations based on the quintiles of football development presented in Table 5.6 shows a clear dominance among UEFA members, while the lowest levels can be seen among North-American (CONCACAF), African (CAF), Asian (AFC), and Oceanian (OFC) nations. Figure 5.10 presents the histograms of FDI value distribution among all six confederations. Geographic (continental) benchmarking points out Japan, Australia, and South Korea being the best reference points for Asian nations; Ghana being a clear leader among African representatives; United States, Costa Rica, Mexico, and Canada—for North America and the Caribbean; Brazil and Argentina—for South America; New Zealand—for Oceania; Germany the reigning world champion—as a benchmark for Europe.

Based on their GDP, nations were classified into 12 peer groups with 15 countries each, except for the last peer group, which included 17 nations (Table 5.7). Three countries (Djibouti, Tahiti, and U.S. Virgin Islands) were eliminated from the dataset due to the inability to obtain valid information on their GDP (PPP) in 2014. In essence, GDP benchmarking on football development shows which countries are able to outperform their economic "odds" as well as the main underperformers. Interestingly enough, most (9 out of 12) of the underperforming nations in football development based on the GDP peer groups were AFC representatives, while UEFA members were 6 times out of 12 classified as benchmark nations for their corresponding peer group. Such a benchmarking process can assist development efforts not only at the national level but at the continental scale as well.

Figure 5.11 shows the five FDI clusters produced using the self-organizing network methodology. The generated clusters do not coincide with FDI quintiles, explained in the previous chapter, nor are they supposed to.

Figure 5.4 CONMEBOL Choropleth Map Based on FDI Values. Created by the authors and IntellSoft Business Group.

Figure 5.5 CONCACAF Choropleth Map Based on FDI Values. Created by the authors and IntellSoft Business Group.

The continental Kohonen maps are provided in the Appendix.

Figure 5.12 indicates an exemplary report-card that can be constructed for each NA based on the results of the Football Development Index. The coloring scheme remains relevant to the one used for the choropleth maps, where dark green signifies a very high value (of 0.8 and higher), while dark red indicates a very low value (0.199 and lower). The graphic breakdown of

Figure 5.6 AFC (Except Australia) Choropleth Map Based on FDI Values. Created by the authors and IntellSoft Business Group.

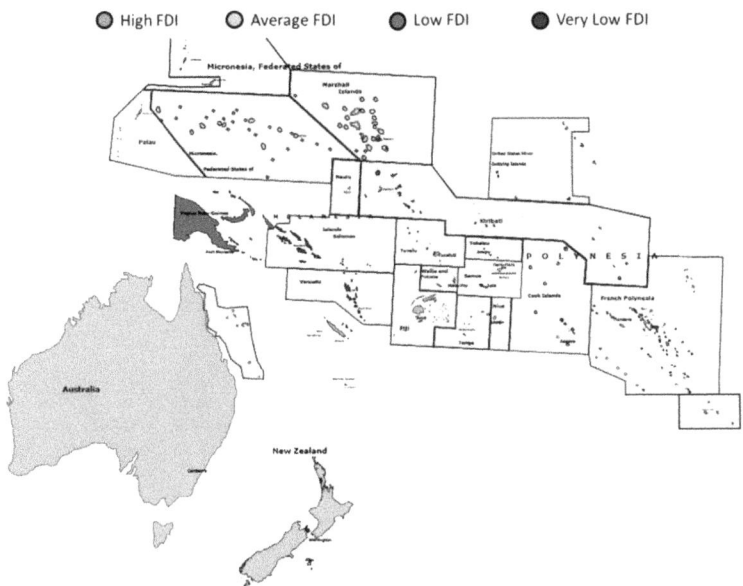

Figure 5.7 OFC with Australia Choropleth Map Based on FDI Values. Created by the authors and IntellSoft Business Group.

58 Chapter 5

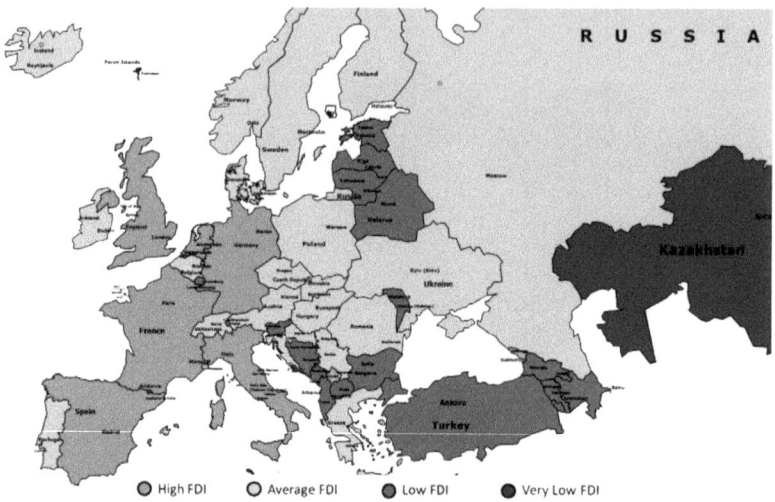

Figure 5.8 UEFA Choropleth Map Based on FDI Values. Created by the authors and IntellSoft Business Group.

Figure 5.9 CAF Choropleth Map Based on FDI Values. Created by the authors and IntellSoft Business Group.

Table 5.6 Distribution of Nations by their Football Development Levels

Football Development Level	FDI Value	Number of Countries	UEFA	CONMEBOL	CONCACAF	AFC	CAF	OFC
Very high	0.8 and higher	0	0	0	0	0	0	0
High	0.799–0.6	8	6	2	0	0	0	0
Average	0.599–0.4	35	22	5	4	3	0	1
Low	0.399–0.2	72	21	3	10	14	22	2
Very low	0.199 and lower	70	4	0	12	23	27	4

Source: Created by the authors

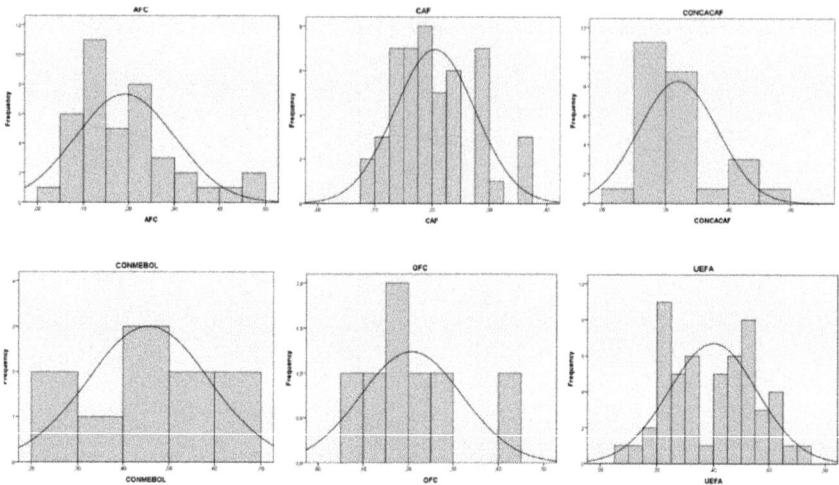

Figure 5.10 Histograms of FDI Value Distributions within all Six Confederations. Created by the authors and IntellSoft Business Group.

Table 5.7 Football Development Benchmark Nations Based on GDP Peer Groups

Peer Group	GDP Range (bil. USD)	Median FDI Value	Benchmark Nation	Underperformer Nation
1	Below 1.69	0.13718	Antigua and Barbuda	Timor-Leste
2	1.70–4.86	0.178283	Cape Verde	Belize
3	4.92–10.68	0.178792	Guinea	Bahamas
4	11.265–14.97	0.20197	Albania	Mongolia
5	15.15–25.94	0.238054	Iceland	Brunei
6	25.97–40.95	0.256156	Paraguay	Uganda
7	41.22–62.09	0.273738	Costa Rica	Turkmenistan
8	62.32–106.74	0.210933	Slovakia	Sri Lanka
9	132.75–230.69	0.335224	Portugal	Bangladesh
10	238.25–387.27	0.324994	Chile	Pakistan
11	417.87–884.73	0.493054	Netherlands	Indonesia
12	1 239.44–17 377.10	0.525059	Germany	India

Source: Created by the authors.

the Germany's FDI results highlights a few "Achilles' heels" in the nation's football development efforts, although it retains the highest position among all countries. Most notable, P3 shows that Germany's match attendance needs more specific attention. An initial thought to this sort of outcome would naturally be: something is definitely wrong. Especially since Germany has

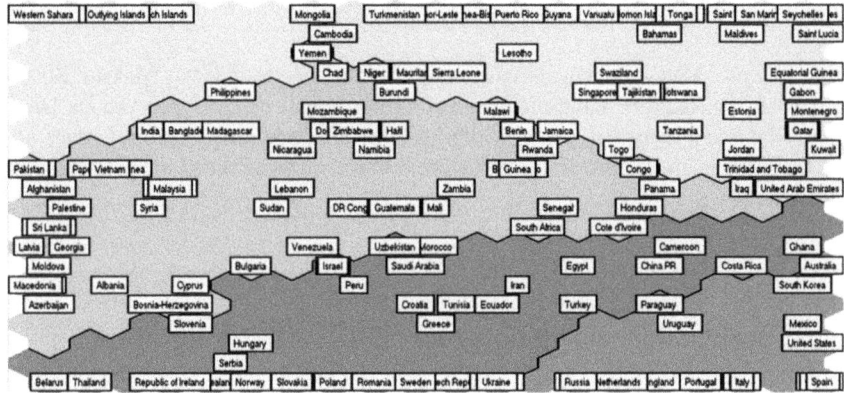

Figure 5.11 FDI Global Kohonen Self-Organizing Map. Created by the authors and IntellSoft Business Group.

Figure 5.12 Exemplary Scorecard of Germany Based on FDI Results. Created by the authors and IntellSoft Business Group.

the highest average match attendance in the world with more than 43,000 spectators per match in the first Bundesliga. However, given the nation's large population this is easily explained. Such a trade-off must be accepted by all largely populated nations, since this gives them the possibility to excel within other indicators and dimensions of the FDI.

An interesting occurrence is the fact that stadium capacity (E2) is also outside of the FDI "green zone" for Germany. Since the constraint of stadium capacity on stadium attendance has already been highlighted in this book, it would be interesting to inductively derive if there is more to this phenomenon in future research projects.

NOTE

1. The provided graphic materials in this chapter were designed by Maksim Kostin and Vladimir Rozin of InterSoft Business Group Russia using Hyper Visions Interface, which is a registered patent within the Russian Federation under reference no. 2009616999 from December 21, 2009. The authors were permitted the publishing of the materials.

Chapter 6

Dependence between Football Rankings and Socioeconomic Indicators

This chapter aims to test the causal relationships between the constructed Football Development Index, on-pitch performance, and socioeconomic indicators.

PREMISE

There is already a large amount of academic literature focusing on the possible effects of exogenous factors on sporting performance and development. Hoffmann, Ging, and Ramasamy (2002) conducted a regression analysis of the FIFA/Coca-Cola ranking and socioeconomic factors in order to estimate whether a country's cultural distinction, demography, and geography are important determinants of international football performance. Per-capita wealth was identified as a significant driver of football success, although only to a certain extent, since overfunding football may disrupt the balance of the game.

This relation between economic growth and sporting success has been raised by several researchers. For example, Houston and Wilson (2002) were among the first to notice the indirect relationship between economic growth and sporting success. More specifically, the authors noted that the relationship is U-shaped, meaning that the economic welfare helps sporting results to a certain point, after which it starts to hamper them. This is explained by the logic that a certain level of economic development serves as an incentive of youngsters to realize their dreams through sports, while children in economically developed nations actually have more opportunities for self-fulfillment within other spheres. Andreff (2006) reviewed the economic determinants of Olympic success and were drawn to the conclusion that a nation's gross domestic product (GDP) and GDP per capita have a big influence on the amount of Olympic podium finishes a country can achieve. Manuel Luiz and Fadal (2011) reviewed the socioeconomic basis of sporting performance on the African continent and also found GDP to be the "overwhelmingly consistent independent variable" in their athletic results models. More so, the authors concluded that on a global scale football success is determined by GDP, climate, and healthcare spending, while African football success is only highly linked with GDP levels. Perhaps the most significant contribution was in Soccernomics by Kuper and Szymanski (2010). The authors analyzed the relationship between a country's national team performance and its GDP per capita. They found countries could be classified into "overperformers" and "underperformers" based on their football/GDP ratio. The top 10 overperforming countries included some well-known football powerhouses, such as Brazil, Germany, and Spain, but also acknowledged the progress of Asian countries such as Iraq and Iran.

Similar research by Leeds and Leeds (2009) determined that, in most cases, countries with higher population and GDP levels produced more positive outcomes. They also found that historical and cultural factors had a role in on-pitch success, since former colonial states were generally unable to vanquish their former colonizers. However, Kuper and Szymanski (2010) label the majority of former colonies as "overperformers." Therefore, future encounters may prove more favorable to the former colonial nations.

It is abundantly clear that football has overcome the boundaries of being merely a sporting event. It now provides an important social responsibility while also being another platform for countries to establish superiority. In order to gain the upper hand sufficient funding is required. This leads to the first premise of this chapter: *a country's wealth is proportional to its positive results on the football pitch.*

Sport, and football in particular, is not the only area government and private funding are allocated. Literacy and healthcare are one of the main global problems, but the status of these issues is extremely variable with regard to geographical position and national wealth. It seems appropriate to determine if there is a link between these factors and sporting success. Better healthcare levels engender healthier and better prepared athletes; higher literacy levels might decrease the amount of young athletes involved in football (or sport in general), because a more literate society may force a child to effectively choose between sport and education. This leads to the second and third research premises: *higher healthcare levels benefit on pitch performance, and higher literacy rates decrease sporting success.*

Apart from the possible social utilities that can be generated through the game of football, business relations also might have a possible link with sports development rates. It is no secret that professional football has evolved into a multibillion dollar industry with complex and interconnected business process (Chadwick, 2009). A priori logic points to the obvious financial supremacy of the football clubs, which represent the football powerhouse nations. The annually conducted Football Money League by Deloitte (2014, 2015, 2016, 2017) showcases an obvious dominance of teams from England, Germany, Spain, Italy, and France. These facts help the authors form the fourth and final premise of the analysis: *higher football development promotes better business relations.*

The analytical framework will select the most representative variables relevant to these hypotheses, eliminate data that could cause analytical bias, test for dependencies and statistical significance, and finally determine the relationship between on-pitch performance and socioeconomic development.

The chapter will be structured accordingly in order to provide an easier interpretation of the conducted analyses and their results:

- Analysis 1: On-pitch performance vs. socioeconomic development
- Analysis 2: Football Development Index vs. socioeconomic development

VARIABLES

Wealth

A country's economic well-being is commonly represented through its GDP. GDP is a standard measure of the value of goods and services produced by a country during a period less the value of imports (OECD, 2015).

Therefore, we adopted per capita GDP to determine a nation's wealth, thereby incorporating the population size. GDP per capita was calculated from World Bank data (World Bank, 2015), and divided the country's GDP by its average yearly population (2006–2013).

Healthcare

A country's level of healthcare reflects its economic development: healthier people are able to contribute more to the economy and vice versa (Well, 2007). A common method to assess the national health level is to estimate a country's average life expectancy. Since healthier people tend to live longer, it is reasonable to assume average lifespan is an indicator of overall health. Therefore, the UN Life Expectancy Index (LEI) was chosen as the healthcare variable.

LEI determines the average age at death for a newborn child using mortality rates over a selected period. The LEI is calculated using the following equation:

$$LEI = \frac{LE-20}{83.2-20}, \tag{6.1}$$

where *LE* is a country's average life expectancy, and the denominator includes the worldwide average maximum (83.2 years) and minimum (20 years) life expectancy. The UN Human Development Report (UNDP, 2015) dataset was employed to extract these data.

Literacy

High literacy level within a country relates to overall socioeconomic development. Illiteracy continues to be a global problem, in most cases caused by the inability for children to access education. Literacy levels may be estimated by the number of years in education (Wagner, 2005). Therefore, the UN Education Index (EI) was adopted to determine national literacy levels.

The EI calculation consists of two components: mean years of schooling and expected years of schooling. Worldwide, the maximum years actually spent within the school system is 15, benchmark that is predicted to be unchanged through to 2025. The maximum expected years of schooling was set to be 18, the duration to complete a master's degree in most countries—as stated in the 2014 Human Development Report Technical Notes (UNDP, 2015).

To illustrate the calculation, consider the educational situation in Costa Rica in 2014:

- Mean years of schooling = 8.37
- Expected years of schooling = 13.5

  1. Mean years of schooling index (MSI) = 8.37/15=0.558
  2. Expected years of schooling index (ESI) = 13.5/18=0.75
  3. Education index = mean of MSI and ESI = (0.558+0.75)/2=0.654

Where a nation fails to provide sufficient valid data, a small number of countries, the UN Human Development Report, which calculates the EI, evaluates the education level using regression. Further details in this regard may be found in the official website of the UN Human Development Report (UNDP, 2015).The EI data was also gathered from that site.

Business Relations

Business relations are a complex phenomenon, which are subsequently difficult to represent quantitatively. To the knowledge of the authors, the Ease of Doing Business Index is the only indicator which attempts to view the development state of business relations of nations from a multidimensional perspective. The detailed description of this indicator may be reviewed in chapter 2.

On-Pitch Performance

There are many determinants of sporting results, from simple medal tallies to complex statistic measurement tools. However, football results of national teams are better represented through ranking systems. This can be stipulated by the fact that international football competitions are played using a group stage and knockout tournament systems. In contrast, national football competitions usually employ a round-robin system (all-play-all), which is arguably the fairest system to determine winners sports. However, a round-robin system requires a considerable amount of time to determine a champion (national football seasons last up to 10 months), while continental and global national team competitions do not go on for more than a month. A knockout system eliminates half of the participants after the conclusion of each round. Subsequently, since teams are mostly randomly paired, there is a fair chance that the final results of such tournament are highly dependent of the draw (Ausloos, Cloots, Gadomski & Vitanov, 2014). Ranking systems are the only way to consolidate and adequately reflect football performance data of national teams, especially since there are 211 members in FIFA, and only up to 32 nations can participate in international tournaments (48 from 2026 for the FIFA World Cup). Therefore this analysis will use the FIFA/Coca-Cola ranking as a proxy for a nation's on-pitch performance. The detailed description of this indicator may be reviewed in chapter 2.

ON-PITCH PERFORMANCE VS. WEALTH, HEALTHCARE, LITERACY, AND BUSINESS RELATIONS

The initial step for the analysis would be to code the variables and estimated normal distributions among the indicators (Table 6.1).

The mean and the standard deviation values of the indicators are presented in Table 6.2. The greater amount of variance can be seen within the FIFA/Coca-Cola ranking and GDP.

The paired correlation matrix is presented in Table 6.3. As we can see, the FIFA/Coca-Cola ranking has statistically significant links with all of the selected socioeconomic indicators. However, the strength of the relationships is moderate at best.

Table 6.1 Indicator Specification of FIFA-SE Analysis

Dimension	Indicator	Coding	Value Type	Scope	Source
On-pitch performance	FIFA/Coca-Cola ranking	FIFA	Scale	2006–2014	FIFA.com
Wealth	GDP per capita (PPP)	GDP	Scale	2006–2014	World Bank
Healthcare	Life Expectancy Index	LEI	Scale	2006–2014	UNDP
Literacy	Education Index	EI	Scale	2006–2014	UNDP

Table 6.2 Mean and Standard Deviation Values of Analysis 1

	FIFA	GDP	LEI	EI
Mean	428.17	14017.41	69.82	0.61
Standard deviation	319.529304	20339.91	9.33527557	0.175784019
Coefficient of variation	0.746	1.45	0.13	0.28

Source: Created by the authors.

Table 6.3 Paired Correlation Matrix of Analysis 1

Indicators	FIFA	GDP	LEI	EI
FIFA	1	0.284149*	0.282874*	0.398757*
GDP	0.284149*	1	0.564019*	0.589104*
LEI	0.282874*	0.564019*	1	0.786618*
EI	0.398757*	0.589104*	0.786618*	1

Source: Created by the authors.
* Significant at p < 0.01

A more detailed understanding of the causal relationships can be achieved through calculating the partial correlation between the indicators. Table 6.4 shows the matrix of the partial correlation coefficients of the selected indicators.

In order to determine the interval estimates of partial correlation coefficients, the Fisher transformation must be applied:

$$z = \frac{1}{2} ln \frac{1+r}{1-r} \tag{6.2}$$

Therefore, the interval estimates will be determined using the following equation:

Dependence between Football Rankings and Socioeconomic Indicators

Table 6.4 Partial Correlation Matrix of Analysis 1

Indicators	FIFA	GDP	LEI	EI
FIFA	1	−0.065	0.050	−0.020
GDP	−0.065	1	0.261	0.297
LEI	0.050	0.261	1	0.547
EI	−0.020	0.297	0.547	1

Source: Created by the authors.

$$z_{1,2} = \frac{1}{2} \ln \frac{1+r}{1-r} \mp \frac{U_{a/2}}{\sqrt{(n-1)-3}} \qquad (6.3)$$

where $n = 187$—number of observations (in this case—number of countries)
 l is the order of correlation coefficient

The derived confidence intervals provide the authors with enough evidence to suggest the statistical significance of partial correlation coefficients. Coefficients which did not pass through zero are statistically insignificant. The others are not statistically significant. Table 6.5 demonstrates that all the coefficients linked with the first factor (FIFA/Coca-Cola ranking) are statistically significant.

If the paired correlation coefficient is significant, and the corresponding partial correlation coefficient is insignificant—this stipulates that the relationship is indirect, because if the influence of other factors is excluded the dependence brakes.

The multiple coefficients characterize the closeness of the linear dependence of all factors at the same time with the result.

In order to obtain these coefficients it is necessary to form matrix of Ri pair correlation coefficients. This matrix should be excluded of the dependent variable.

Then the multiple correlation coefficients are given by:

$$R = \sqrt{1 - \frac{|R_0|}{|R|}} \qquad (6.4)$$

where $|R|$—Determinant of pair correlation coefficients signs $\{x1, \ldots, xn\}$, $|Ro|$—Determinant of pair correlations signs $\{x0, x1, \ldots, Xm\}$.

The results of the calculation of the multiple correlation coefficients are presented in Table 6.6.

After determining the values of the m-coefficients they have to be tested for statistical significance. In order to do so we have to form a statistic hypothesis H_0:

Table 6.5 Dataset of Confidence Intervals

Indicator	Controlled By	r	z	z Down	z up	r Down	r Up
FIFA	GDP	-0.06536	-0.06546	-0.21114	0.080226	-0.20806	0.080054
FIFA	LEI	0.049726	0.049767	-0.09592	0.19545	-0.09562	0.192999
FIFA	EI	-0.02037	-0.02037	-0.16605	0.125315	-0.16454	0.124663
GDP	LEI	0.261019	0.267201	0.121518	0.412884	0.120924	0.390919
GDP	EI	0.297177	0.30642	0.160737	0.452103	0.159367	0.423626
LEI	EI	0.546729	0.613704	0.468021	0.759387	0.436599	0.640716

Source: Created by the authors.

Table 6.6 The Multiple Correlation Coefficients of the Analyzed Variables

Indicator	Multiple Correlation Coefficients
FIFA	0.40849
GDP	0.709848
LEI	0.937088
EI	0.965306

Source: Created by the authors.

$$R_{YX}=0 \iff H_1: R_{yx} \neq 0. \quad (6.5)$$

Estimated statistics:

$$F = \frac{R_{YX}^2}{1-R_{YX}^2} \cdot \frac{n-p-1}{p} \quad (6.6)$$

where $n = 187$—number of countries,
$p = m - 1 = 4$, where m—number of factors.
Tabulated value:

$$F_{table} = F(\alpha; p; n-p-1) = F(0{,}05; 5; 187-5-1) = 2.26 \quad (6.7)$$

If $F_{calc} > F_{table}$, then hypothesis H_0 is accepted, the coefficient of multiple correlation statistically equals to zero, the regression equation is not significant, the model is inapplicable.

If $F_{calc} > F_{table}$ then hypothesis H_0 is rejected. This indicates that the multiple correlation coefficient is statistically different from zero, thus, the regression equation is significant.

The multiple correlation coefficient and determination coefficient are codependent $D = R2yx$ The determination coefficient shows the variability of the Y variable which is caused by the factors used in the analysis. The results of the calculations are presented in Table 6.7.

The third (Life expectancy) and fourth (Education) factors show high levels of multiple correlation; consequently they can be used as dependent

Table 6.7 Summary Matrix of Analysis 1

Dependent Factor	Multiple Correlation Coefficient (R)	R^2	F_{calc}	F_{table}
FIFA	0.40849	0.166864	7.250289	2.264029
GDP	0.709848	0.503884	36.76682	
LEI	0.937088	0.878133	260.8454	
EI	0.965306	0.931816	494.7202	

Source: Created by the authors.

variable in the modeling of these factors. Moreover, the dependent variable model can be used for those factors that have multiple correlation coefficients closer to 1 and use the remaining as explanatory factors. For example, X5 = α1*X1+α2*X2+α3*X3+α4*X4, where α1, α2, α3, and α4 are the coefficients of the model.

FOOTBALL DEVELOPMENT INDEX VS. WEALTH, HEALTHCARE, LITERACY, AND BUSINESS RELATIONS

This section will test whether the designed Football Development Index has tighter relations with socioeconomic indicators. This analysis is forced to incorporate rank values of all indicators, since the Ease of Doing Business Index only provides rank values as its quantitative representation. Therefore, the Pearson paired correlation coefficients are inapplicable for this sort of dataset and Spearman and Kendall coefficients have to be applied.

Both Spearman and Kendall correlation coefficients possess the same qualities as the Pearson coefficient. Their values vary from –1 to +1. The Spearman correlation coefficient is calculated using the following equation:

$$r_s = 1 - \frac{6 \times \sum_{i=1}^{n} d_i^2}{n^3 - n} \tag{6.8}$$

where d_i—the difference between the rank values of n observations

The Kendall correlation coefficient can be calculated using the following equation:

$$\tau = \frac{4 \times \sum_{i=1}^{n-1} R_i}{n(n-1)} - 1 \tag{6.9}$$

where n—the number of observations (number of cross-compared rank values);

R_i—the number of ranks in the second variation row, which are larger than the corresponding rank value and the ranks values below.

The significance test for Kendall's correlation coefficient is based on comparing the calculated "tau" value with its critical values:

$$\tau_a(n) = z_{1-\frac{a}{2}} \sqrt{\frac{2(2n+5)}{9n(n+1)}} \tag{6.10}$$

Table 6.8 presents the Spearman and Kendall correlation coefficients of the Football Development Index compared to socioeconomic indicators.

Table 6.8 Spearman and Kendall Correlation Coefficients of the Football Development Index Compared to Socioeconomic Indicators (2013 data)

FDI vs.	Spearman Correlation	Kendall Correlation
GDP	0.338446*	0.224069*
Life Expectancy Index	0.341817*	0.23545*
Education Index	0.359546*	0.245419*
Ease of Doing Business Index	0.300467*	0.204810*

Source: Created by the authors.
* Statistically significant at $p < 0.01$.

All of the calculated correlations are statistically significant and indicate a moderate relationship between the indicators. The correlation levels seem to become stronger when a larger time scope is used, which can be explained by the control of year-to-year fluctuations.

Table 6.9 clearly demonstrates that the correlation levels have increased compared to the results of the 2013 data. However, the relation can still be regarded as moderate at best. The problem could be with data heterogeneity. A similar problem was identified by Kuper and Szymanski (2010) when assessing the relation between GDP and on-pitch performance.

Table 6.10 demonstrates the Spearman and Kendall correlation coefficients on 2013 data for the FDI of UEFA and Table 6.10 showing the results of the test on 2006–2013 data.

Table 6.9 Spearman and Kendall Correlation Coefficients of the Football Development Index Compared to Socioeconomic Indicators (2006–2013 data)

FDI vs.	Spearman Correlation	Kendall Correlation
GDP	0.473947*	0.362601*
Life Expectancy Index	0.420197*	0.328079*
Education Index	0.466252*	0.355557*
Ease of Doing Business Index	0.466735*	0.354893*

Source: Created by the authors.
* Statistically significant at $p < 0.01$.

Table 6.10 Spearman and Kendall Correlation Coefficients of the Football Development Index of UEFA Compared to Socioeconomic Indicators (2006–2013 data)

FDI of UEFA vs.	Spearman Correlation	Kendall Correlation
GDP	0.617558**	0.519735**
Life Expectancy Index	0.563241**	0.419455**
Education Index	0.318049**	0.363330**
Ease of Doing Business Index	−0.058533**	0.071111**

Source: Created by the authors.
* Statistically significant at $p < 0.01$.

The causal relationship between the FDI and socioeconomic indicators seems to be more evident on a European scale. However, still, the Education Index and the Ease of Doing Business Index show little evidence of strong linkage.

MAIN FINDINGS

The results of Analysis 1 show that a country's FIFA ranking position has a statistically significant correlation with the analyzed indicators of socioeconomic development. The strongest correlation link with football performance was found for Education Index and Human Development Index. However, these links cannot be considered sufficient to form an indisputable conclusion about a strong (or even at least) a moderate relation between the indicators. Then again, such a result does not exclude the possible existence of a close dependency between a country's socioeconomic level and youth and grassroots football, sports infrastructure, and technical/methodological proficiency of football staff—factors that are in no way incorporated into the official FIFA rankings.

After a further analysis of the selected variables it was determined that the Education Index actually has the highest correlation with the FIFA ranking out of all the other socioeconomic indicators. The authors' ex-ante analysis proposed a different outcome. It is difficult for the authors to logically form an explanation for this phenomenon. But in terms of interpreting the results of the analysis it should not be forgotten that a correlation does not guarantee a causal relationship between the variables, but only shows that their trends are similar and there may be an additional third factor that affects both variables. Such a scenario is quite possible in case of the correlation between the FIFA ranking and Education Index.

A country's wealth which is determined by the authors in its GDP per capita along with a country's healthcare levels showed the weakest correlation levels with the FIFA ranking out of the whole variable dataset. These findings could be regarded as the main surprise of the analysis, since once again the authors' ex-ante prognosis and plain logic stipulate the increase in sporting achievements with population income growth and good healthcare. However, using only the sport results of the main men's national teams, it is impossible to estimate the volume and efficiency of using funds invested in football. It is similarly impossible to draw conclusions about the general level of health in countries on the results of 11 footballers who go out on the field, defending the banners of their country.

So, on the one hand, based on the derived weak dependency levels between sports and nonsports indicators it is fair to say that a country's socioeconomic environment does not play the most important role in the ability of its male national A-team to achieve results. The findings of Analysis 1 showcase that it is pointless to argue that the increase in the level of human development or GDP is directly reflected on football results. However, as stated before, the FIFA ranking has serious limitations regarding the amount of variables it includes. Therefore, it would be a huge misconception to regard the data from the FIFA rankings as an actual representation of overall football development.

The authors do not deny that national team results are an important indicator of the development of football, but it is also not the only variable which characterizes football development. A more justified assumption would be that the men's national team is the cornerstone of a multilevel football "pyramid." Therefore, a lack of top-tier sport achievements may not always be an indicator of a weak football development situation in a given country. The foundation of the so-called pyramid consists of infrastructure—which is one of the key components of youth-talent preparation. Well-built management systems, proper governance of grassroots football, implementation of football programs, and various information databases are also the core components of any well-functioning football system. However, even the proper functioning of the above-mentioned components of the pyramid may not always lead to on-pitch success of the senior national football men's team, at least not momentarily. This is exactly the reason why the FIFA ranking is not an adequate indicator of overall football development, since it only provides a single perspective of a complex matter, though it is still a measure of football performance.

Therefore, it would be a logical assumption to state that the comparison between more complex and variable inclusive factors of football development with socioeconomic indicators could highlight more significant causality relationships. Such an outcome shows the need for the creation of a specialized system of assessing the development level of global football, which takes into account not only the performances indicators. Improving data samples and the variables involved in the analysis could help achieve more robust and descriptive results. Consequently, the findings of the analysis point us to the conclusion that little or no statistical relationship between football results and socioeconomic development can be found, which is somewhat contradictory to previous studies. Consequently, the findings of Analysis 1 point directly to the necessity of conducting Analysis 2. Analysis 2 tested the causal relationships between the football development represented through the Football Development Index and socioeconomic indicators. The analysis included calculation for data over a single period (2013), several periods (2006–2013), a single period for UEFA members (2013), and several periods for UEFA members (2006–2013).

The findings cautiously confirm the hypotheses arisen from the findings of Analysis 1. The calculated Spearman and Kendall correlation coefficients indicate the presence of statistically significant and moderate relationships between the FDI and socioeconomic indexes. The strongest link can be found between the GDP values of UEFA members and their FDI, which coincides with the hypothesis that football development can be (partially) explained by the economic growth. Contrary to the findings of Analysis 1, the Education Index showed the least strength in relation to the FDI compared to the other components of Human Development Index: GDP and the Life Expectancy Index.

Conclusion

Football fans have always been raising questions such as why some nations are able to produce one talented generation of football after another, while others consistently fall to the bottom of the global football pyramid. As the famous football player and now TV expert Gary Lineker once said, "22 men chase a ball for 90 minutes and at the end, the Germans always win".

Previous research in the field of global football development has attempted to introduce models for predicting match and tournament outcomes (e.g., Scelles & Andreff, 2014). However, these studies do not provide us with the answer to the question: "why Germany?" Why have Costa Rica, Chile, Iceland, Wales, and others have been able to show such progress both on and off the pitch, while more economically stable nations such as China, India, and Indonesia are still unable to pose a threat to the long-standing football powerhouses?

Another perspective which could be of interest to the global football stakeholders is the factors which contribute the most to the success. Competitive balance must be ensured, since it is one of the key concepts that ensure the long-term viability of football tournaments (Michie & Oughton, 2004). Therefore, it is imperative that continental leaders, such as Germany in Europe, and Brazil and Argentina in South America, do not increase too much the gap between the continental football "peloton."

The authors of this book have attempted to introduce a practically oriented methodology that could provide (at least to some extent) answers to the above-mentioned questions. This book attempted to introduce a composite indicator of football development that would include three dimensions and 12 indicators. The conducted literature review on sports development and football performance allowed the authors to form the definition of football development, to the assessment of which the Football Development Index is firstly dedicated. The calculation methodology of the FDI was predominantly based on the recommendations of Nardo et al. (2008), while also following the globally accepted practices of renowned index systems (Human Development Index, Social Progress Index, and others).

After due deliberation the authors selected a min-max normalization method, which was dictated by the need to use a "mixed" aggregation approach with dimension scores being aggregated linearly and the composite indicator calculated via geometric aggregation. The selection of the equal weighting method was explained by the fairly similar results produced by using more sophisticated methods (i.e., frequency-based and statistical approaches). The FDI also allows to benchmark the best football development practices through geographic and economic attributes. This way, NAs will be able to see beyond the conventional powerhouse nations as global benchmarks and review the development practices adopted in countries with similar exogenous environments.

The findings of this paper could serve as an additional incentive to those FIFA members who might not be able to compete with the modern football powerhouses on the pitch but who are devoted to developing grassroots and youth football. Therefore, the funding allocation which is annually conducted by FIFA may be more objectively distributed not only to those who need it the most but also to those who will most efficiently use this funding. The FDI might also be decomposed and "localized" at continental and national levels, while being adapted to address the needs of a specific confederation or FA. The possible comparison with other composite indicators of socioeconomic development and more sophisticated benchmarking criteria could help provide a better understanding of global football development policies.

The authors fully comprehend that the proposed methodology is open to criticism due to some of the assumptions made within the model construction phase. The rationale behind selecting some of the indicators was largely stipulated by the ability to obtain relevant and trustworthy data.

One of the essential aspects of this research is not the overall position of a given country in the final ranking or in one of the three group rankings, but the actual description and interpretation of the results. Based on the findings of the research, National FAs will have a decretive layout of their current level of football development. Besides they will be able to establish the causality relations and dependencies among the selected criteria and other factors based on the country's socioeconomic, cultural, and historical peculiarities (Vorobyev, Zarova, Solntsev, Osokin, & Zhulevich, 2016). Therefore, this ranking system demonstrates a generalized approach toward data consolidation which can afterwards be modified and adapted by any given football entity to fit and emphasize its own context.

On a global scale the differentiation among FIFA member-countries by the level of football development will allow all members of the football community to analyze the evolution of certain countries, determine the factors contributing to their success, and establish the main reason for the downfalls. Thus, the FDI provides an overview of modern football evolution, gives an opportunity to benchmark the best global development practices, and avoid the past mistakes.

Some findings might strike the general public as being surprising and difficult to comprehend. Again we refer to the cases of India and China with match attendance. Namibia, Faroe Islands, Montserrat, Barbados, Anguilla, Bermuda, Vanuatu, Aruba, Cook Islands, and San Marino are more commonly known as football outsiders yet all of these countries are ranked in the top 20 based on the criterion of "percentage of population playing football" which might draw the football community to the assumption that football superiority is not only assessed through World Cup victories or million dollar transfer fees for players.

The conducted research and calculation model will lay out the road map of future projects in this scientific area, diversifying the definition of football development while shifting the false-based prejudices of assessing global football. Along with the interpretation of each criteria group a description of the selected criteria and the calculation model itself must be further detailed and given proper evaluation and argumentation. Deriving the dependencies among the three criteria groups will also become a key component of this research's development.

Since modern football requires fast-paced evolvement, the identification of its key development factors may prove vital for the future prosperity of the game and help development managers to rationalize their activities focusing particularly on the most important performance indicators.

The other side of the project's future development should be focused on pursuing the socioeconomic application of the FDI results. Sports, having long an integral part of a country's social development policy, is also regarded as one of its main performance indicators. Therefore, having formed a scientifically based tool for materializing and giving a specific value to the term "level of football development," it may be given a practical application by various nonsports related parties. Since there are numerous widely renowned socioeconomic rankings such as the gender-inequality index, the Gini index, and the various versions of the Human Development Index—their results may be compared and cross-analyzed with the findings of the Football Development Index, thus becoming a stepping-stone for a whole new chapter in the issue of the debated hypothesis about a direct connection between sporting and socioeconomic success.

Conclusion

Therefore, the main course of future development of this scientific problem will evolve around establishing a direct line of communication with NAs, continental federations, sports marketing as well as consulting agencies and cooperating various research institutions for examining the problems of modern football development more in-depth. This will enable to verify the current statistical database and enhance and modify the methodology. This book does not dare to fixate the views of the football and scientific communities on a single manner of assessing the development of the world's most beloved game. Even more so, this written contribution aims to shed a light on a topical matter of making decisions within global football in a more data-informed and scientifically objective manner. Therefore, this book explicitly acknowledges that the path of quantifying football policy has only begun and that expanding the current database, introducing better suited methodological features, and generating new practical implications of quantification tools such as the FDI should be among the main priorities of football development stakeholders.

Appendix A
"On-Pitch Performance" Dimension Results

Appendix A

Table A.1 "On-Pitch Performance" Dimension Results

Country	National Teams	Clubs	FIFA Ranking (Female)	FIFA Ranking (Male)	On-pitch Performance
Afghanistan	0.00	0.00	0.00	0.11	*0.03*
Albania	0.00	0.06	0.00	0.31	*0.09*
Algeria	0.04	0.11	0.00	0.55	*0.17*
Andorra	0.00	0.01	0.00	0.00	*0.00*
Antigua and Barbuda	0.00	0.00	0.00	0.20	*0.05*
Argentina	0.58	0.61	0.74	0.89	*0.71*
Armenia	0.00	0.03	0.00	0.25	*0.07*
Australia	0.22	0.22	0.90	0.18	*0.38*
Austria	0.03	0.28	0.78	0.50	*0.40*
Azerbaijan	0.00	0.14	0.00	0.12	*0.06*
Bahamas	0.00	0.00	0.00	0.01	*0.00*
Bahrain	0.01	0.05	0.00	0.14	*0.05*
Bangladesh	0.00	0.00	0.00	0.05	*0.01*
Barbados	0.00	0.00	0.00	0.10	*0.03*
Belarus	0.01	0.22	0.68	0.19	*0.27*
Belgium	0.08	0.38	0.79	0.82	*0.52*
Belize	0.00	0.00	0.00	0.04	*0.01*
Benin	0.01	0.00	0.00	0.21	*0.05*
Bolivia	0.00	0.29	0.00	0.21	*0.13*
Bosnia-Herzegovina	0.01	0.08	0.00	0.47	*0.14*
Botswana	0.00	0.00	0.00	0.18	*0.04*
Brazil	1.00	0.78	0.90	0.76	*0.86*
Brunei	0.00	0.00	0.00	0.00	*0.00*
Bulgaria	0.00	0.18	0.00	0.29	*0.12*
Burkina Faso	0.03	0.00	0.00	0.30	*0.08*
Burundi	0.00	0.00	0.00	0.13	*0.03*
Cambodia	0.00	0.00	0.00	0.03	*0.01*
Cameroon	0.14	0.07	0.00	0.38	*0.15*
Canada	0.14	0.18	0.90	0.16	*0.35*
Cape Verde	0.00	0.00	0.00	0.40	*0.10*
Central African Republic	0.00	0.00	0.00	0.10	*0.02*
Chad	0.00	0.00	0.00	0.10	*0.02*
Chile	0.14	0.57	0.72	0.59	*0.51*
China PR	0.13	0.21	0.86	0.19	*0.35*
Colombia	0.19	0.49	0.78	0.84	*0.57*
Comoros	0.00	0.00	0.00	0.04	*0.01*
Congo	0.02	0.11	0.00	0.30	*0.11*
Costa Rica	0.17	0.17	0.73	0.58	*0.41*
Cote d'Ivoire	0.08	0.04	0.00	0.48	*0.15*
Croatia	0.07	0.25	0.00	0.55	*0.22*
Cuba	0.02	0.00	0.00	0.15	*0.04*
Cyprus	0.00	0.24	0.00	0.21	*0.11*
Czech Republic	0.12	0.31	0.76	0.57	*0.44*
Denmark	0.05	0.21	0.85	0.46	*0.40*
Dominica	0.00	0.00	0.00	0.02	*0.01*
Dominican Republic	0.00	0.00	0.00	0.18	*0.04*
DR Congo	0.01	0.12	0.00	0.31	*0.11*
Ecuador	0.08	0.35	0.68	0.49	*0.40*

Table A.1 "On-Pitch Performance" Dimension Results *(Continued)*

Country	National Teams	Clubs	FIFA Ranking (Female)	FIFA Ranking (Male)	On-pitch Performance
Egypt	0.13	0.27	0.00	0.30	*0.18*
El Salvador	0.03	0.11	0.00	0.20	*0.09*
England	0.22	0.85	0.91	0.60	*0.64*
Equatorial Guinea	0.01	0.00	0.00	0.14	*0.04*
Estonia	0.00	0.04	0.00	0.22	*0.07*
Ethiopia	0.01	0.02	0.00	0.16	*0.05*
Faroe Islands	0.00	0.04	0.00	0.18	*0.05*
Fiji	0.00	0.10	0.00	0.01	*0.03*
Finland	0.01	0.09	0.82	0.27	*0.30*
France	0.42	0.55	0.96	0.67	*0.65*
Gabon	0.01	0.00	0.00	0.29	*0.07*
Gambia	0.02	0.00	0.00	0.05	*0.02*
Georgia	0.00	0.10	0.00	0.13	*0.06*
Germany	0.61	0.82	1.00	1.00	*0.86*
Ghana	0.23	0.03	0.67	0.41	*0.33*
Greece	0.06	0.34	0.00	0.49	*0.22*
Grenada	0.00	0.00	0.00	0.07	*0.02*
Guatemala	0.03	0.13	0.00	0.26	*0.11*
Guinea	0.00	0.00	0.00	0.41	*0.10*
Guinea-Bissau	0.00	0.00	0.00	0.12	*0.03*
Guyana	0.00	0.01	0.00	0.05	*0.02*
Haiti	0.00	0.02	0.00	0.26	*0.07*
Honduras	0.07	0.13	0.00	0.26	*0.12*
Hong Kong	0.00	0.08	0.00	0.07	*0.04*
Hungary	0.03	0.12	0.72	0.36	*0.31*
Iceland	0.00	0.09	0.84	0.44	*0.34*
India	0.00	0.06	0.00	0.04	*0.02*
Indonesia	0.00	0.10	0.00	0.07	*0.04*
Iran	0.10	0.28	0.00	0.33	*0.18*
Iraq	0.05	0.14	0.00	0.18	*0.09*
Israel	0.00	0.23	0.00	0.45	*0.17*
Italy	0.39	0.67	0.86	0.64	*0.64*
Jamaica	0.01	0.00	0.00	0.26	*0.07*
Japan	0.41	0.26	0.96	0.32	*0.49*
Jordan	0.01	0.12	0.00	0.22	*0.09*
Kazakhstan	0.01	0.11	0.00	0.11	*0.06*
Kenya	0.00	0.00	0.00	0.15	*0.04*
Kuwait	0.01	0.17	0.00	0.14	*0.08*
Kyrgyzstan	0.00	0.00	0.00	0.08	*0.02*
Laos	0.00	0.00	0.00	0.07	*0.02*
Latvia	0.00	0.05	0.00	0.19	*0.06*
Lebanon	0.00	0.07	0.00	0.13	*0.05*
Lesotho	0.00	0.00	0.00	0.14	*0.03*
Liberia	0.00	0.00	0.00	0.15	*0.04*
Libya	0.01	0.01	0.00	0.25	*0.07*
Liechtenstein	0.00	0.06	0.00	0.12	*0.05*
Lithuania	0.00	0.05	0.00	0.20	*0.06*
Luxembourg	0.00	0.06	0.00	0.13	*0.05*

Table A.1 "On-Pitch Performance" Dimension Results *(Continued)*

Country	National Teams	Clubs	FIFA Ranking (Female)	FIFA Ranking (Male)	On-pitch Performance
Macedonia	0.00	0.06	0.00	0.18	*0.06*
Madagascar	0.00	0.00	0.00	0.09	*0.02*
Malawi	0.00	0.00	0.00	0.20	*0.05*
Malaysia	0.00	0.06	0.00	0.08	*0.03*
Maldives	0.00	0.03	0.00	0.12	*0.04*
Mali	0.03	0.11	0.00	0.35	*0.12*
Malta	0.00	0.05	0.00	0.09	*0.03*
Mauritania	0.00	0.00	0.00	0.12	*0.03*
Mauritius	0.00	0.00	0.00	0.02	*0.00*
Mexico	0.36	0.44	0.80	0.53	*0.53*
Moldova	0.00	0.11	0.00	0.14	*0.06*
Mongolia	0.00	0.00	0.00	0.01	*0.00*
Montenegro	0.00	0.06	0.00	0.31	*0.09*
Morocco	0.05	0.15	0.00	0.22	*0.11*
Mozambique	0.00	0.00	0.00	0.19	*0.05*
Namibia	0.00	0.00	0.00	0.17	*0.04*
Nepal	0.00	0.00	0.00	0.02	*0.01*
Netherlands	0.24	0.43	0.89	0.80	*0.59*
New Zealand	0.11	0.16	0.84	0.12	*0.31*
Nicaragua	0.00	0.04	0.00	0.04	*0.02*
Niger	0.00	0.01	0.00	0.15	*0.04*
Nigeria	0.37	0.14	0.75	0.38	*0.41*
Northern Ireland	0.00	0.05	0.00	0.35	*0.10*
Norway	0.06	0.16	0.89	0.29	*0.35*
Oman	0.01	0.05	0.00	0.20	*0.06*
Pakistan	0.00	0.00	0.00	0.02	*0.01*
Palestine	0.00	0.00	0.00	0.15	*0.04*
Panama	0.04	0.12	0.00	0.31	*0.12*
Papua New Guinea	0.00	0.09	0.68	0.00	*0.19*
Paraguay	0.21	0.56	0.00	0.25	*0.25*
Peru	0.01	0.33	0.00	0.32	*0.17*
Philippines	0.00	0.00	0.00	0.12	*0.03*
Poland	0.04	0.23	0.75	0.39	*0.35*
Portugal	0.30	0.65	0.71	0.67	*0.58*
Puerto Rico	0.00	0.10	0.00	0.06	*0.04*
Qatar	0.00	0.20	0.00	0.19	*0.10*
Republic of Ireland	0.04	0.06	0.77	0.30	*0.29*
Romania	0.00	0.28	0.73	0.59	*0.40*
Russia	0.17	0.52	0.82	0.45	*0.49*
Rwanda	0.00	0.00	0.00	0.28	*0.07*
Saint Kitts and Nevis	0.00	0.00	0.00	0.15	*0.04*
Saint Lucia	0.00	0.00	0.00	0.11	*0.03*
Saint Vincent and the Grenadines	0.00	0.00	0.00	0.14	*0.04*
Samoa	0.00	0.02	0.00	0.01	*0.01*
San Marino	0.00	0.01	0.00	0.03	*0.01*

Table A.1 "On-Pitch Performance" Dimension Results *(Continued)*

Country	National Teams	Clubs	FIFA Ranking (Female)	FIFA Ranking (Male)	On-pitch Performance
São Tomé and Príncipe	0.00	0.00	0.00	0.04	*0.01*
Saudi Arabia	0.04	0.39	0.00	0.18	*0.15*
Scotland	0.01	0.19	0.82	0.42	*0.36*
Senegal	0.07	0.00	0.00	0.42	*0.12*
Serbia	0.05	0.15	0.70	0.41	*0.33*
Seychelles	0.00	0.00	0.00	0.03	*0.01*
Sierra Leone	0.00	0.00	0.00	0.21	*0.05*
Singapore	0.00	0.06	0.00	0.07	*0.03*
Slovakia	0.05	0.12	0.68	0.51	*0.34*
Slovenia	0.03	0.15	0.00	0.36	*0.13*
Solomon Islands	0.03	0.04	0.00	0.03	*0.02*
South Africa	0.06	0.07	0.00	0.33	*0.11*
South Korea	0.28	0.38	0.84	0.27	*0.44*
Spain	0.60	1.00	0.86	0.66	*0.78*
Sri Lanka	0.00	0.00	0.00	0.04	*0.01*
Sudan	0.00	0.13	0.00	0.17	*0.07*
Suriname	0.00	0.00	0.00	0.06	*0.02*
Swaziland	0.00	0.00	0.00	0.06	*0.02*
Sweden	0.15	0.19	0.92	0.37	*0.41*
Switzerland	0.13	0.37	0.84	0.63	*0.49*
Syria	0.02	0.08	0.00	0.08	*0.05*
Tajikistan	0.01	0.00	0.00	0.12	*0.03*
Tanzania	0.00	0.00	0.00	0.18	*0.04*
Thailand	0.04	0.15	0.76	0.11	*0.26*
Timor-Leste	0.00	0.00	0.00	0.02	*0.01*
Togo	0.02	0.00	0.00	0.30	*0.08*
Tonga	0.00	0.01	0.00	0.00	*0.00*
Trinidad and Tobago	0.02	0.07	0.68	0.32	*0.27*
Tunisia	0.05	0.36	0.00	0.50	*0.23*
Turkey	0.11	0.35	0.00	0.35	*0.20*
Turkmenistan	0.00	0.00	0.00	0.09	*0.02*
Uganda	0.00	0.00	0.00	0.25	*0.06*
Ukraine	0.12	0.45	0.81	0.49	*0.47*
United Arab Emirates	0.06	0.20	0.00	0.22	*0.12*
United States	0.51	0.21	0.99	0.48	*0.55*
Uruguay	0.27	0.45	0.00	0.66	*0.34*
Uzbekistan	0.04	0.20	0.00	0.26	*0.13*
Vanuatu	0.00	0.10	0.00	0.01	*0.03*
Venezuela	0.02	0.22	0.00	0.21	*0.11*
Vietnam	0.00	0.09	0.75	0.12	*0.24*
Wales	0.00	0.03	0.75	0.43	*0.30*
Yemen	0.00	0.01	0.00	0.04	*0.01*
Zambia	0.01	0.01	0.00	0.36	*0.10*
Zimbabwe	0.00	0.01	0.00	0.17	*0.05*

Source: Created by the authors based on AFC (2017); FIFA (2015); Global Football Ranks (2017); UEFA (2017).

Appendix B
"Popularity" Dimensions Results

Table B.1 'Popularity' Dimensions Results

Country	Participation	Registered clubs	Attendance	Popularity
Afghanistan	0.34	0.36	0.25	0.32
Albania	0.51	0.58	0.46	0.51
Algeria	0.56	0.34	0.23	0.38
Andorra	0.32	0.31	0.87	0.50
Antigua and Barbuda	0.37	0.25	0.85	0.49
Argentina	0.63	0.69	0.23	0.52
Armenia	0.48	0.32	0.45	0.41
Australia	0.52	0.74	0.27	0.51
Austria	0.71	0.74	0.36	0.60
Azerbaijan	0.46	0.42	0.35	0.41
Bahamas	0.34	0.30	0.67	0.44
Bahrain	0.10	0.28	0.53	0.30
Bangladesh	0.59	0.64	0.13	0.45
Barbados	0.62	0.53	0.70	0.62
Belarus	0.47	0.34	0.35	0.39
Belgium	0.62	0.71	0.33	0.55
Belize	0.35	0.31	0.67	0.44
Benin	0.42	0.31	0.34	0.35
Bolivia	0.55	0.60	0.34	0.49
Bosnia-Herzegovina	0.50	0.64	0.43	0.52
Botswana	0.45	0.29	0.49	0.41
Brazil	0.69	0.86	0.12	0.56
Brunei	0.07	0.17	0.65	0.30
Bulgaria	0.49	0.56	0.37	0.47
Burkina Faso	0.47	0.27	0.30	0.35
Burundi	0.44	0.36	0.34	0.38
Cambodia	0.28	0.22	0.31	0.27
Cameroon	0.48	0.37	0.27	0.38
Canada	0.67	0.85	0.24	0.59
Cape Verde	0.47	0.41	0.63	0.50
Central African Republic	0.45	0.38	0.41	0.41
Chad	0.44	0.19	0.32	0.32
Chile	0.79	0.82	0.29	0.63
China PR	0.52	0.48	0.00	0.33
Colombia	0.64	0.66	0.22	0.51
Comoros	0.31	0.04	0.59	0.31
Congo	0.46	0.31	0.41	0.40
Costa Rica	0.86	0.46	0.41	0.58
Cote d'Ivoire	0.50	0.37	0.28	0.39
Croatia	0.62	0.73	0.42	0.59
Cuba	0.69	0.47	0.33	0.50
Cyprus	0.46	0.42	0.58	0.49
Czech Republic	0.69	0.81	0.34	0.61
Denmark	0.65	0.78	0.39	0.61
Dominica	0.30	0.26	0.88	0.48
Dominican Republic	0.52	0.47	0.34	0.44
DR Congo	0.54	0.48	0.19	0.40
Ecuador	0.62	0.37	0.31	0.43

Table B.1 'Popularity' Dimensions Results *(Continued)*

Country	Participation	Registered Clubs	Attendance	Popularity
Egypt	0.54	0.44	0.17	*0.39*
El Salvador	0.58	0.26	0.37	*0.40*
England	0.69	1.00	0.21	*0.63*
Equatorial Guinea	0.29	0.16	0.59	*0.35*
Estonia	0.39	0.45	0.53	*0.46*
Ethiopia	0.56	0.50	0.17	*0.41*
Faroe Islands	0.60	0.42	0.94	*0.65*
Fiji	0.44	0.64	0.57	*0.55*
Finland	0.57	0.35	0.39	*0.44*
France	0.65	0.89	0.20	*0.58*
Gabon	0.39	0.29	0.50	*0.40*
Gambia	0.37	0.26	0.49	*0.37*
Georgia	0.49	0.44	0.41	*0.45*
Germany	0.90	0.89	0.18	*0.66*
Ghana	0.51	0.39	0.26	*0.39*
Greece	0.61	0.85	0.33	*0.60*
Grenada	0.33	0.23	0.83	*0.46*
Guatemala	0.75	0.32	0.30	*0.46*
Guinea	0.45	0.34	0.33	*0.37*
Guinea-Bissau	0.40	0.23	0.50	*0.38*
Guyana	0.49	0.42	0.59	*0.50*
Haiti	0.50	0.46	0.34	*0.43*
Honduras	0.52	0.42	0.35	*0.43*
Hong Kong	0.31	0.21	0.37	*0.30*
Hungary	0.54	0.76	0.34	*0.55*
Iceland	0.54	0.53	0.69	*0.59*
India	0.49	0.60	0.00	*0.36*
Indonesia	0.53	0.17	0.10	*0.27*
Iran	0.45	0.25	0.18	*0.29*
Iraq	0.33	0.26	0.24	*0.28*
Israel	0.43	0.45	0.36	*0.42*
Italy	0.68	0.87	0.20	*0.58*
Jamaica	0.51	0.50	0.45	*0.49*
Japan	0.57	0.57	0.15	*0.43*
Jordan	0.27	0.31	0.38	*0.32*
Kazakhstan	0.43	0.17	0.30	*0.30*
Kenya	0.57	0.49	0.22	*0.43*
Kuwait	0.16	0.20	0.44	*0.27*
Kyrgyzstan	0.30	0.32	0.39	*0.34*
Laos	0.25	0.21	0.38	*0.28*
Latvia	0.41	0.36	0.49	*0.42*
Lebanon	0.56	0.41	0.40	*0.46*
Lesotho	0.47	0.38	0.48	*0.44*
Liberia	0.42	0.22	0.41	*0.35*
Libya	0.47	0.33	0.38	*0.39*
Liechtenstein	0.37	0.14	0.98	*0.50*
Lithuania	0.46	0.28	0.45	*0.40*
Luxembourg	0.53	0.49	0.62	*0.55*

Table B.1 'Popularity' Dimensions Results *(Continued)*

Country	Participation	Registered Clubs	Attendance	Popularity
Macedonia	0.43	0.60	0.49	*0.51*
Madagascar	0.49	0.37	0.27	*0.38*
Malawi	0.44	0.23	0.30	*0.32*
Malaysia	0.37	0.27	0.25	*0.30*
Maldives	0.39	0.37	0.68	*0.48*
Mali	0.67	0.32	0.30	*0.43*
Malta	0.41	0.37	0.65	*0.48*
Mauritania	0.42	0.28	0.43	*0.38*
Mauritius	0.48	0.33	0.54	*0.45*
Mexico	0.69	0.35	0.15	*0.40*
Moldova	0.47	0.32	0.43	*0.41*
Mongolia	0.21	0.00	0.45	*0.22*
Montenegro	0.06	0.41	0.61	*0.36*
Morocco	0.57	0.48	0.25	*0.43*
Mozambique	0.48	0.33	0.26	*0.36*
Namibia	1.00	0.36	0.47	*0.61*
Nepal	0.34	0.27	0.26	*0.29*
Netherlands	0.71	0.80	0.30	*0.60*
New Zealand	0.86	0.51	0.41	*0.59*
Nicaragua	0.61	0.68	0.38	*0.56*
Niger	0.44	0.30	0.29	*0.34*
Nigeria	0.58	0.12	0.13	*0.27*
Northern Ireland	0.45	0.70	0.50	*0.55*
Norway	0.68	0.83	0.40	*0.63*
Oman	0.18	0.21	0.42	*0.27*
Pakistan	0.41	0.43	0.12	*0.32*
Palestine	0.26	0.47	0.41	*0.38*
Panama	0.44	0.60	0.43	*0.49*
Papua New Guinea	0.37	0.52	0.37	*0.42*
Paraguay	0.36	0.72	0.37	*0.48*
Peru	0.62	0.65	0.25	*0.51*
Philippines	0.40	0.19	0.17	*0.25*
Poland	0.59	0.77	0.23	*0.53*
Portugal	0.54	0.75	0.34	*0.55*
Puerto Rico	0.54	0.30	0.43	*0.42*
Qatar	0.00	0.08	0.48	*0.19*
Republic of Ireland	0.64	0.92	0.41	*0.66*
Romania	0.57	0.72	0.29	*0.52*
Russia	0.58	0.80	0.14	*0.51*
Rwanda	0.45	0.30	0.33	*0.36*
Saint Kitts and Nevis	0.29	0.36	0.92	*0.52*
Saint Lucia	0.36	0.34	0.76	*0.49*
Saint Vincent and the Grenadines	0.44	0.42	0.82	*0.56*
Samoa	0.15	0.42	0.75	*0.44*
San Marino	0.36	0.27	1.00	*0.54*
São Tomé and Príncipe	0.26	0.08	0.75	*0.36*

Appendix B

Table B.1   **'Popularity' Dimensions Results** *(Continued)*

Country	Participation	Registered Clubs	Attendance	Popularity
Saudi Arabia	0.31	0.31	0.26	*0.29*
Scotland	0.61	0.93	0.40	*0.65*
Senegal	0.52	0.37	0.31	*0.40*
Serbia	0.56	0.74	0.37	*0.56*
Seychelles	0.32	0.24	0.84	*0.47*
Sierra Leone	0.47	0.11	0.38	*0.32*
Singapore	0.43	0.23	0.39	*0.35*
Slovakia	0.70	0.74	0.40	*0.61*
Slovenia	0.49	0.55	0.49	*0.51*
Solomon Islands	0.36	0.56	0.62	*0.52*
South Africa	0.74	0.39	0.21	*0.45*
South Korea	0.42	0.24	0.21	*0.29*
Spain	0.63	0.90	0.22	*0.58*
Sri Lanka	0.36	0.50	0.28	*0.38*
Sudan	0.53	0.44	0.23	*0.40*
Suriname	0.45	0.24	0.63	*0.44*
Swaziland	0.39	0.31	0.54	*0.41*
Sweden	0.70	0.82	0.35	*0.62*
Switzerland	0.60	0.71	0.36	*0.56*
Syria	0.36	0.34	0.28	*0.32*
Tajikistan	0.26	0.20	0.36	*0.27*
Tanzania	0.10	0.33	0.22	*0.22*
Thailand	0.41	0.28	0.20	*0.30*
Timor-Leste	0.09	0.03	0.55	*0.22*
Togo	0.43	0.31	0.37	*0.37*
Tonga	0.24	0.56	0.83	*0.54*
Trinidad and Tobago	0.49	0.38	0.53	*0.47*
Tunisia	0.52	0.43	0.33	*0.43*
Turkey	0.54	0.69	0.18	*0.47*
Turkmenistan	0.27	0.05	0.40	*0.24*
Uganda	0.48	0.42	0.23	*0.38*
Ukraine	0.60	0.20	0.23	*0.34*
United Arab Emirates	0.13	0.13	0.35	*0.20*
United States	0.73	0.70	0.09	*0.51*
Uruguay	0.57	0.37	0.44	*0.46*
Uzbekistan	0.42	0.35	0.25	*0.34*
Vanuatu	0.55	0.63	0.71	*0.63*
Venezuela	0.57	0.54	0.25	*0.45*
Vietnam	0.43	0.09	0.17	*0.23*
Wales	0.51	0.44	0.45	*0.47*
Yemen	0.31	0.27	0.27	*0.28*
Zambia	0.62	0.58	0.31	*0.50*
Zimbabwe	0.52	0.45	0.31	*0.43*

Source: Created by the authors based on FIFA (2006); European-football-statistics.co.uk (2015); Worldfootball.net (2017).

Appendix C
"Environment" Dimensions Results

Table C.1 "Environment" Dimensions Results

Country	Youth Players	Stadium Capacity	Coaches	FIFA Referees	National Squads	Environment
Afghanistan	0.42	0.26	0.31	0.13	0.42	0.31
Albania	0.83	0.56	0.18	0.25	0.32	0.43
Algeria	0.68	0.45	0.33	0.35	0.42	0.45
Andorra	0.92	0.24	0.31	0.10	0.42	0.40
Antigua and Barbuda	0.74	0.71	0.92	0.08	0.21	0.53
Argentina	0.70	0.54	0.31	0.90	0.63	0.62
Armenia	0.79	0.50	0.00	0.30	0.37	0.39
Australia	0.92	0.45	0.32	0.65	0.42	0.55
Austria	0.98	0.47	0.47	0.60	0.53	0.61
Azerbaijan	0.74	0.51	0.17	0.48	0.58	0.49
Bahamas	0.55	0.53	0.39	0.08	0.37	0.38
Bahrain	0.67	0.79	0.70	0.48	0.32	0.59
Bangladesh	0.54	0.13	0.10	0.30	0.11	0.24
Barbados	0.86	0.30	0.56	0.13	0.16	0.40
Belarus	0.52	0.45	0.15	0.38	0.53	0.40
Belgium	0.96	0.53	0.41	0.78	0.74	0.68
Belize	0.61	0.58	0.55	0.05	0.00	0.36
Benin	0.30	0.42	0.42	0.45	0.05	0.33
Bolivia	0.61	0.47	0.38	0.55	0.11	0.42
Bosnia-Herzegovina	0.84	0.58	0.29	0.38	0.47	0.51
Botswana	0.63	0.53	0.52	0.35	0.26	0.46
Brazil	0.78	0.49	0.21	1.00	0.53	0.60
Brunei	0.58	0.82	0.44	0.25	0.05	0.43
Bulgaria	0.69	0.64	0.11	0.70	0.11	0.45
Burkina Faso	0.43	0.37	0.39	0.33	0.11	0.32
Burundi	0.37	0.22	0.36	0.35	0.21	0.30
Cambodia	0.28	0.35	0.26	0.23	0.00	0.22
Cameroon	0.38	0.41	0.39	0.60	0.42	0.44

Appendix C

Canada	0.87	0.34	0.23	0.25	0.58	0.46
Cape Verde	0.79	0.52	0.72	0.30	0.00	0.47
Central African Republic	0.40	0.24	0.39	0.25	0.00	0.26
Chad	0.20	0.27	0.31	0.30	0.00	0.22
Chile	0.77	0.38	0.31	0.73	0.68	0.57
China PR	0.52	0.38	0.12	0.80	0.42	0.45
Colombia	0.66	0.41	0.30	0.60	0.42	0.48
Comoros	0.25	0.51	0.51	0.23	0.00	0.30
Congo	0.41	0.44	0.50	0.35	0.11	0.36
Costa Rica	0.49	0.33	0.37	0.60	0.47	0.45
Cote d'Ivoire	0.39	0.34	0.39	0.43	0.37	0.38
Croatia	0.83	0.53	0.28	0.68	0.42	0.55
Cuba	0.47	0.30	0.29	0.30	0.21	0.31
Cyprus	0.83	0.68	0.21	0.50	0.32	0.51
Czech Republic	0.99	0.43	0.33	0.68	0.53	0.59
Denmark	0.97	0.55	0.43	0.50	0.63	0.62
Dominica	0.68	0.75	0.71	0.05	0.00	0.44
Dominican Republic	0.61	0.29	0.37	0.15	0.00	0.28
DR Congo	0.45	0.31	0.29	0.38	0.05	0.30
Ecuador	0.41	0.47	0.37	0.70	0.11	0.41
Egypt	0.35	0.41	0.27	0.60	0.26	0.38
El Salvador	0.62	0.44	0.39	0.53	0.16	0.42
England	0.90	0.50	0.59	0.63	0.74	0.67
Equatorial Guinea	0.45	0.74	0.66	0.35	0.05	0.45
Estonia	0.64	0.53	0.61	0.35	0.68	0.56
Ethiopia	0.35	0.21	0.22	0.40	0.05	0.25
Faroe Islands	0.97	0.92	0.29	0.08	0.37	0.52
Fiji	0.95	0.63	0.33	0.35	0.37	0.52
Finland	0.89	0.48	0.44	0.58	0.74	0.62
France	0.93	0.46	0.31	0.85	0.79	0.67
Gabon	0.57	0.72	0.61	0.33	0.05	0.45
Gambia	0.43	0.52	0.43	0.30	0.16	0.37

Table C.1 "Environment" Dimensions Results (Continued)

Country	Youth Players	Stadium Capacity	Coaches	FIFA Referees	National Squads	Environment
Georgia	0.62	0.56	0.21	0.33	0.37	0.42
Germany	0.93	0.43	0.32	0.78	0.74	0.64
Ghana	0.39	0.41	0.37	0.55	0.21	0.39
Greece	0.93	0.51	0.26	0.68	0.42	0.56
Grenada	0.66	0.64	0.78	0.03	0.00	0.42
Guatemala	0.61	0.35	0.29	0.30	0.16	0.34
Guinea	0.44	0.24	0.45	0.45	0.16	0.35
Guinea-Bissau	0.27	0.44	0.51	0.20	0.00	0.28
Guyana	0.65	0.06	0.46	0.28	0.00	0.29
Haiti	0.48	0.20	0.41	0.23	0.05	0.27
Honduras	0.68	0.48	0.42	0.35	0.21	0.43
Hong Kong	0.33	0.47	0.14	0.40	0.05	0.28
Hungary	0.79	0.55	0.36	0.68	0.21	0.52
Iceland	0.97	0.69	0.25	0.33	0.74	0.60
India	0.45	0.29	0.03	0.40	0.05	0.25
Indonesia	0.29	0.42	0.11	0.25	0.21	0.26
Iran	0.82	0.52	0.32	0.83	0.42	0.58
Iraq	0.37	0.51	0.36	0.45	0.16	0.37
Israel	0.68	0.53	0.48	0.53	0.21	0.49
Italy	0.83	0.48	0.42	0.90	0.63	0.65
Jamaica	0.66	0.35	0.50	0.40	0.21	0.42
Japan	0.81	0.45	0.25	0.75	0.58	0.57
Jordan	0.35	0.49	0.53	0.43	0.16	0.39
Kazakhstan	0.49	0.48	0.03	0.58	0.32	0.38
Kenya	0.47	0.32	0.25	0.43	0.00	0.29
Kuwait	0.33	0.73	0.57	0.50	0.05	0.44
Kyrgyzstan	0.48	0.44	0.41	0.35	0.53	0.44
Laos	0.22	0.42	0.41	0.13	0.00	0.24

Latvia	0.53	0.45	0.11	0.40	0.37	0.37
Lebanon	0.48	0.48	0.37	0.50	0.00	0.37
Lesotho	0.77	0.31	0.48	0.28	0.00	0.37
Liberia	0.44	0.17	0.45	0.20	0.53	0.36
Libya	0.36	0.52	0.45	0.35	0.05	0.35
Liechtenstein	0.94	0.92	0.24	0.00	0.47	0.52
Lithuania	0.59	0.52	0.13	0.40	0.53	0.43
Luxembourg	0.98	0.64	0.21	0.25	0.53	0.52
Macedonia	0.75	0.61	0.16	0.40	0.42	0.47
Madagascar	0.43	0.25	0.26	0.48	0.00	0.28
Malawi	0.42	0.33	0.38	0.38	0.21	0.34
Malaysia	0.26	0.58	0.28	0.48	0.16	0.35
Maldives	0.73	0.47	0.67	0.20	0.00	0.41
Mali	0.22	0.31	0.34	0.45	0.16	0.29
Malta	0.86	0.56	0.19	0.33	0.26	0.44
Mauritania	0.36	0.09	0.43	0.25	0.16	0.26
Mauritius	0.72	0.41	0.31	0.30	0.00	0.35
Mexico	0.53	0.35	0.23	0.78	0.63	0.51
Moldova	0.46	0.45	0.10	0.33	0.63	0.39
Mongolia	0.52	0.14	0.29	0.08	0.00	0.21
Montenegro	0.74	1.00	0.34	0.25	0.42	0.55
Morocco	0.65	0.48	0.30	0.58	0.32	0.46
Mozambique	0.46	0.34	0.33	0.40	0.00	0.30
Namibia	0.46	0.00	0.31	0.25	0.26	0.26
Nepal	0.36	0.29	0.18	0.35	0.21	0.28
Netherlands	1.00	0.44	0.34	0.75	0.79	0.66
New Zealand	0.63	0.30	0.27	0.30	0.42	0.38
Nicaragua	0.80	0.15	0.23	0.15	0.00	0.27
Niger	0.22	0.35	0.34	0.23	0.00	0.23
Nigeria	0.28	0.33	0.24	0.70	0.53	0.41
Northern Ireland	0.87	0.61	0.39	0.23	0.63	0.55
Norway	0.99	0.49	0.40	0.58	0.26	0.54

Table C.1 "Environment" Dimensions Results *(Continued)*

Country	Youth Players	Stadium Capacity	Coaches	FIFA Referees	National Squads	Environment
Oman	0.62	0.68	0.60	0.45	0.21	0.51
Pakistan	0.40	0.29	0.06	0.20	0.47	0.28
Palestine	0.64	0.59	0.07	0.28	0.00	0.32
Panama	0.33	0.42	0.52	0.38	0.11	0.35
Papua New Guinea	0.85	0.27	0.11	0.33	0.00	0.31
Paraguay	0.91	0.59	0.49	0.63	0.26	0.58
Peru	0.70	0.46	0.31	0.68	0.11	0.45
Philippines	0.34	0.25	0.24	0.28	0.00	0.22
Poland	0.87	0.50	0.31	0.75	0.84	0.66
Portugal	0.79	0.63	0.30	0.75	0.84	0.66
Puerto Rico	0.59	0.41	0.34	0.10	0.00	0.29
Qatar	0.80	0.90	0.75	0.33	0.32	0.62
Republic of Ireland	0.97	0.48	0.49	0.43	1.00	0.67
Romania	0.64	0.57	0.24	0.78	0.63	0.57
Russia	0.75	0.42	0.23	0.88	0.63	0.58
Rwanda	0.34	0.33	0.43	0.40	0.21	0.34
Saint Kitts and Nevis	0.80	0.83	1.00	0.10	0.00	0.55
Saint Lucia	0.71	0.58	0.74	0.15	0.00	0.44
Saint Vincent and the Grenadines	0.85	0.71	0.81	0.08	0.21	0.53
Samoa	0.80	0.46	0.57	0.03	0.00	0.37
SanMarino	0.88	0.75	0.26	0.08	0.47	0.49
São Tomé and Príncipe	0.39	0.51	0.69	0.15	0.00	0.35
Saudi Arabia	0.39	0.55	0.38	0.40	0.26	0.40
Scotland	0.80	0.58	0.43	0.50	0.79	0.62
Senegal	0.81	0.40	0.41	0.55	0.11	0.46
Serbia	0.83	0.54	0.29	0.63	0.53	0.56
Seychelles	0.76	0.76	0.69	0.25	0.05	0.50
Sierra Leone	0.29	0.40	0.45	0.18	0.05	0.27
Singapore	0.43	0.36	0.36	0.38	0.32	0.37

Slovakia	1.00	0.42	0.38	0.63	0.68	0.62
Slovenia	0.77	0.52	0.55	0.55	0.53	0.58
Solomon Islands	0.79	0.52	0.46	0.38	0.11	0.45
South Africa	0.94	0.41	0.24	0.53	0.32	0.49
South Korea	0.40	0.58	0.34	0.63	0.68	0.53
Spain	0.81	0.53	0.32	0.90	0.47	0.61
Sri Lanka	0.64	0.25	0.25	0.23	0.58	0.39
Sudan	0.00	0.30	0.28	0.53	0.00	0.22
Suriname	0.74	0.55	0.52	0.13	0.00	0.39
Swaziland	0.49	0.36	0.46	0.20	0.32	0.37
Sweden	0.96	0.49	0.37	0.65	0.74	0.64
Switzerland	0.89	0.54	0.35	0.63	0.68	0.62
Syria	0.56	0.46	0.31	0.35	0.16	0.37
Tajikistan	0.28	0.52	0.44	0.30	0.32	0.37
Tanzania	0.61	0.58	0.44	0.28	0.16	0.41
Thailand	0.36	0.46	0.24	0.63	1.00	0.54
Timor-Leste	0.14	0.36	0.51	0.00	0.00	0.20
Togo	0.39	0.47	0.48	0.35	0.21	0.38
Tonga	0.94	0.46	0.53	0.10	0.00	0.40
Trinidad and Tobago	0.70	0.56	0.59	0.13	0.05	0.41
Tunisia	0.61	0.49	0.43	0.65	0.21	0.48
Turkey	0.61	0.47	0.32	0.75	0.74	0.58
Turkmenistan	0.10	0.60	0.44	0.30	0.00	0.29
Uganda	0.46	0.24	0.33	0.33	0.00	0.27
Ukraine	0.86	0.46	0.06	0.75	0.79	0.58
United Arab Emirates	0.52	0.72	0.57	0.60	0.26	0.53
United States	0.80	0.42	0.17	0.60	0.84	0.57
Uruguay	0.70	0.66	0.51	0.75	0.58	0.64
Uzbekistan	0.49	0.46	0.37	0.63	0.21	0.43
Vanuatu	0.70	0.13	0.40	0.23	0.00	0.29
Venezuela	0.48	0.43	0.30	0.50	0.21	0.38
Vietnam	0.28	0.42	0.22	0.50	0.00	0.28

Table C.1 "Environment" Dimensions Results (Continued)

Country	Youth Players	Stadium Capacity	Coaches	FIFA Referees	National Squads	Environment
Wales	0.87	0.55	0.51	0.25	0.74	0.58
Yemen	0.31	0.43	0.24	0.30	0.05	0.26
Zambia	0.40	0.38	0.36	0.35	0.11	0.32
Zimbabwe	0.50	0.35	0.34	0.33	0.05	0.31

Source: Created by the authors based on FIFA (2006, 2015); Worldstadiums.com (2017).

Appendix D
Football Development Index Results

Table D.1 Football Development Index Results

Country	On-pitch Performance	Popularity	Environment	Football Development Index
Afghanistan	0.03	0.32	0.31	0.14
Albania	0.09	0.51	0.43	0.27
Algeria	0.17	0.38	0.45	0.31
Andorra	0.00	0.50	0.40	0.08
Antigua and Barbuda	0.05	0.49	0.53	0.23
Argentina	0.71	0.52	0.62	0.61
Armenia	0.07	0.41	0.39	0.22
Australia	0.38	0.51	0.55	0.48
Austria	0.40	0.60	0.61	0.53
Azerbaijan	0.06	0.41	0.49	0.23
Bahamas	0.00	0.44	0.38	0.08
Bahrain	0.05	0.30	0.59	0.21
Bangladesh	0.01	0.45	0.24	0.11
Barbados	0.03	0.62	0.40	0.18
Belarus	0.27	0.39	0.40	0.35
Belgium	0.52	0.55	0.68	0.58
Belize	0.01	0.44	0.36	0.11
Benin	0.05	0.35	0.33	0.18
Bolivia	0.13	0.49	0.42	0.30
Bosnia-Herzegovina	0.14	0.52	0.51	0.34
Botswana	0.04	0.41	0.46	0.20
Brazil	0.86	0.56	0.60	0.66
Brunei	0.00	0.30	0.43	0.05
Bulgaria	0.12	0.47	0.45	0.29
Burkina Faso	0.08	0.35	0.32	0.21
Burundi	0.03	0.38	0.30	0.16
Cambodia	0.01	0.27	0.22	0.07
Cameroon	0.15	0.38	0.44	0.29
Canada	0.35	0.59	0.46	0.45
Cape Verde	0.10	0.50	0.47	0.29
Central African Republic	0.02	0.41	0.26	0.14
Chad	0.02	0.32	0.22	0.12
Chile	0.51	0.63	0.57	0.57
China PR	0.35	0.33	0.45	0.37
Colombia	0.57	0.51	0.48	0.52
Comoros	0.01	0.31	0.30	0.10
Congo	0.11	0.40	0.36	0.25
Costa Rica	0.41	0.58	0.45	0.48
Cote d'Ivoire	0.15	0.39	0.38	0.28
Croatia	0.22	0.59	0.55	0.41
Cuba	0.04	0.50	0.31	0.19
Cyprus	0.11	0.49	0.51	0.30
Czech Republic	0.44	0.61	0.59	0.54
Denmark	0.40	0.61	0.62	0.53
Dominica	0.01	0.48	0.44	0.11

Table D.1 Football Development Index Results *(Continued)*

Country	On-pitch Performance	Popularity	Environment	Football Development Index
Dominican Republic	0.04	0.44	0.28	0.18
DR Congo	0.11	0.40	0.30	0.24
Ecuador	0.40	0.43	0.41	0.41
Egypt	0.18	0.39	0.38	0.30
El Salvador	0.09	0.40	0.42	0.25
England	0.64	0.63	0.67	0.65
Equatorial Guinea	0.04	0.35	0.45	0.18
Estonia	0.07	0.46	0.56	0.26
Ethiopia	0.05	0.41	0.25	0.17
Faroe Islands	0.05	0.65	0.52	0.27
Fiji	0.03	0.55	0.52	0.20
Finland	0.30	0.44	0.62	0.43
France	0.65	0.58	0.67	0.63
Gabon	0.07	0.40	0.45	0.24
Gambia	0.02	0.37	0.37	0.13
Georgia	0.06	0.45	0.42	0.22
Germany	0.86	0.66	0.64	0.71
Ghana	0.33	0.39	0.39	0.37
Greece	0.22	0.60	0.56	0.42
Grenada	0.02	0.46	0.42	0.15
Guatemala	0.11	0.46	0.34	0.26
Guinea	0.10	0.37	0.35	0.24
Guinea-Bissau	0.03	0.38	0.28	0.15
Guyana	0.02	0.50	0.29	0.13
Haiti	0.07	0.43	0.27	0.20
Honduras	0.12	0.43	0.43	0.28
Hong Kong	0.04	0.30	0.28	0.15
Hungary	0.31	0.55	0.52	0.44
Iceland	0.34	0.59	0.60	0.49
India	0.02	0.36	0.25	0.13
Indonesia	0.04	0.27	0.26	0.14
Iran	0.18	0.29	0.58	0.31
Iraq	0.09	0.28	0.37	0.21
Israel	0.17	0.42	0.49	0.32
Italy	0.64	0.58	0.65	0.63
Jamaica	0.07	0.49	0.42	0.24
Japan	0.49	0.43	0.57	0.49
Jordan	0.09	0.32	0.39	0.22
Kazakhstan	0.06	0.30	0.38	0.19
Kenya	0.04	0.43	0.29	0.17
Kuwait	0.08	0.27	0.44	0.21
Kyrgyzstan	0.02	0.34	0.44	0.14
Laos	0.02	0.28	0.24	0.10
Latvia	0.06	0.42	0.37	0.21
Lebanon	0.05	0.46	0.37	0.20
Lesotho	0.03	0.44	0.37	0.18

Table D.1 Football Development Index Results *(Continued)*

Country	On-pitch Performance	Popularity	Environment	Football Development Index
Liberia	0.04	0.35	0.36	0.17
Libya	0.07	0.39	0.35	0.21
Liechtenstein	0.05	0.50	0.52	0.23
Lithuania	0.06	0.40	0.43	0.22
Luxembourg	0.05	0.55	0.52	0.24
Macedonia	0.06	0.51	0.47	0.24
Madagascar	0.02	0.38	0.28	0.13
Malawi	0.05	0.32	0.34	0.18
Malaysia	0.03	0.30	0.35	0.15
Maldives	0.04	0.48	0.41	0.20
Mali	0.12	0.43	0.29	0.25
Malta	0.03	0.48	0.44	0.19
Mauritania	0.03	0.38	0.26	0.14
Mauritius	0.00	0.45	0.35	0.09
Mexico	0.53	0.40	0.51	0.47
Moldova	0.06	0.41	0.39	0.22
Mongolia	0.00	0.22	0.21	0.05
Montenegro	0.09	0.36	0.55	0.26
Morocco	0.11	0.43	0.46	0.28
Mozambique	0.05	0.36	0.30	0.17
Namibia	0.04	0.61	0.26	0.19
Nepal	0.01	0.29	0.28	0.08
Netherlands	0.59	0.60	0.66	0.62
New Zealand	0.31	0.59	0.38	0.41
Nicaragua	0.02	0.56	0.27	0.14
Niger	0.04	0.34	0.23	0.14
Nigeria	0.41	0.27	0.41	0.36
Northern Ireland	0.10	0.55	0.55	0.31
Norway	0.35	0.63	0.54	0.49
Oman	0.06	0.27	0.51	0.21
Pakistan	0.01	0.32	0.28	0.08
Palestine	0.04	0.38	0.32	0.17
Panama	0.12	0.49	0.35	0.27
Papua New Guinea	0.19	0.42	0.31	0.29
Paraguay	0.25	0.48	0.58	0.41
Peru	0.17	0.51	0.45	0.34
Philippines	0.03	0.25	0.22	0.12
Poland	0.35	0.53	0.66	0.50
Portugal	0.58	0.55	0.66	0.60
Puerto Rico	0.04	0.42	0.29	0.17
Qatar	0.10	0.19	0.62	0.23
Republic of Ireland	0.29	0.66	0.67	0.50
Romania	0.40	0.52	0.57	0.49
Russia	0.49	0.51	0.58	0.53
Rwanda	0.07	0.36	0.34	0.21
Saint Kitts and Nevis	0.04	0.52	0.55	0.22
Saint Lucia	0.03	0.49	0.44	0.18
Saint Vincent and the Grenadines	0.04	0.56	0.53	0.22

Table D.1 Football Development Index Results *(Continued)*

Country	On-pitch Performance	Popularity	Environment	Football Development Index
Samoa	0.01	0.44	0.37	0.10
San Marino	0.01	0.54	0.49	0.13
São Tomé and Príncipe	0.01	0.36	0.35	0.11
Saudi Arabia	0.15	0.29	0.40	0.26
Scotland	0.36	0.65	0.62	0.52
Senegal	0.12	0.40	0.46	0.28
Serbia	0.33	0.56	0.56	0.47
Seychelles	0.01	0.47	0.50	0.12
Sierra Leone	0.05	0.32	0.27	0.17
Singapore	0.03	0.35	0.37	0.16
Slovakia	0.34	0.61	0.62	0.51
Slovenia	0.13	0.51	0.58	0.34
Solomon Islands	0.02	0.52	0.45	0.18
South Africa	0.11	0.45	0.49	0.29
South Korea	0.44	0.29	0.53	0.41
Spain	0.78	0.58	0.61	0.65
Sri Lanka	0.01	0.38	0.39	0.11
Sudan	0.07	0.40	0.22	0.19
Suriname	0.02	0.44	0.39	0.14
Swaziland	0.02	0.41	0.37	0.13
Sweden	0.41	0.62	0.64	0.55
Switzerland	0.49	0.56	0.62	0.55
Syria	0.05	0.32	0.37	0.18
Tajikistan	0.03	0.27	0.37	0.15
Tanzania	0.04	0.22	0.41	0.16
Thailand	0.26	0.30	0.54	0.35
Timor-Leste	0.01	0.22	0.20	0.06
Togo	0.08	0.37	0.38	0.22
Tonga	0.00	0.54	0.40	0.09
Trinidad and Tobago	0.27	0.47	0.41	0.37
Tunisia	0.23	0.43	0.48	0.36
Turkey	0.20	0.47	0.58	0.38
Turkmenistan	0.02	0.24	0.29	0.12
Uganda	0.06	0.38	0.27	0.19
Ukraine	0.47	0.34	0.58	0.45
United Arab Emirates	0.12	0.20	0.53	0.24
United States	0.55	0.51	0.57	0.54
Uruguay	0.34	0.46	0.64	0.47
Uzbekistan	0.13	0.34	0.43	0.26
Vanuatu	0.03	0.63	0.29	0.18
Venezuela	0.11	0.45	0.38	0.27
Vietnam	0.24	0.23	0.28	0.25
Wales	0.30	0.47	0.58	0.43
Yemen	0.01	0.28	0.26	0.10
Zambia	0.10	0.50	0.32	0.25
Zimbabwe	0.05	0.43	0.31	0.18

Source: Created by the authors.

Bibliography

[dataset] FIFA. (2006). Big count. Retrieved March 3, 2016, from http://www.fifa.com/worldfootball/bigcount/index.html

[dataset] FIFA. (2015b). Tournaments. Retrieved November 30, 2016, from http://www.fifa.com/tournaments/archive/index.html

[dataset] World Bank. (2017). GDP ranking. Retrieved January 30, 2017, from http://data.worldbank.org/data-catalog/GDP-ranking-table.

AFC. (2017). *Club competitions ranking.* [online] The-afc.com. Retrieved July 24, 2017, from http://www.the-afc.com/afc-club-competitions-ranking.

AIBA. (2017). *National federations.* [online] AIBA. Retrieved July 24, 2017, from http://www.aiba.org/national-federations/.

Alkire, S. & Santos, M. E. (2010). Acute multidimensional poverty: A new index for developing countries. *OPHI Working Paper Series, 38.*

———., & Eli, K. (2010). *Multidimensional poverty in developing countries: A measure using existing international data.* mimeo.

———., & Foster, J. (2011). Counting and multidimensional poverty measurement. *Journal of Public Economics, 95*(7), 476–487.

———., Roche, J. M., Seth, S., & Sumner, A. (2015). Identifying the poorest people and groups: Strategies using the Global Multidimensional Poverty Index. *Journal of International Development, 27*(3), 362–387.

Alm, J., Solberg, H. A., Storm, R. K., & Jakobsen, T. G. (2016). Hosting major sports events: The challenge of taming white elephants. *Leisure Studies, 35*(5), 564–582.

Amorose, A. J. (2007). Coaching effectiveness: Exploring the relationship between coaching behavior and self-determined motivation. In Hagger, M., Chatzisarantis, N.L.D. (eds.) *Intrinsic Motivation and Self-determination in Exercise and Sport,* 209–227. Champaign, IL: Human Kinetics.

Anand, S., & Sen, A. (1997). Concepts or human development and poverty! A multidimensional perspective. United Nations Development Programme. *Poverty and Human Development: Human Development Papers,* 1–20.

———. (2000). The income component of the human development index. *Journal of Human Development, 1*(1), 83–106.

Andreff, W. (2006). Comparative advantage of nations. In Andreff W., Szymanski S. (eds.) *Handbook on the Economics of Sport*, 331. Cheltenham: Edward Elgar Publishing

———., & Scelles, N. (2015). Walter C. Neale 50 years after: Beyond competitive balance, the league standing effect tested with French football data. *Journal of Sports Economics, 16*(8), 819–834.

Andrikopoulos, A., & Kaimenakis, N. (2009). Introducing FOrNeX: A composite index for the intangible resources of the football club. *International Journal of Sport Management and Marketing, 5*(3), 251–266.

Ángeles Oviedo-García, M., Muñoz-Expósito, M., Castellanos-Verdugo, M., & Sancho-Mejías, M. (2014). Metric proposal for customer engagement in Facebook. *Journal of Research in Interactive Marketing, 8*(4), 327–344.

Angelini, G., Bernini, C., & Guizzardi, A. (2013). Comparing weighting systems in the measurement of subjective well-being. *Statistica, 73*(2), 143.

Angulo, R., Díaz, Y., & Pardo, R. (2016). The Colombian multidimensional poverty index: Measuring poverty in a public policy context. *Social Indicators Research, 127*(1), 1–38.

Antonopoulos, I. S., Perkoulidis, G., Logothetis, D., & Karkanias, C. (2014). Ranking municipal solid waste treatment alternatives considering sustainability criteria using the analytical hierarchical process tool. *Resources, Conservation and Recycling, 86*, 149–159.

Arbone, J., Corke, T., & Moisiadis, F. (2016). The Rugby League Prediction Model: Using an Elo-based approach to predict the outcome of National Rugby League (Nrl) Matches. *International Educational Scientific Research Journal, 2*(5), 26–30

Ausloos, M., Cloots, R., Gadomski, A., & Vitanov, N. K. (2014). Ranking structures and rank–rank correlations of countries: The FIFA and UEFA cases. *International Journal of Modern Physics C, 25*(11), 1450060.

Babic, Z., & Plazibat, N. (1998). Ranking of enterprises based on multicriterial analysis. *International Journal of Production Economics, 56*, 29–35.

Bairner, A. (2004). Creating a soccer strategy for Northern Ireland: Reflections on football governance in small European countries. *Soccer & Society, 5*(1), 27–42.

Bandura, R. (2008). A survey of composite indices measuring country performance: 2008 Update. New York: United Nations Development Programme, Office of Development Studies (UNDP/ODS Working Paper).

Baranzini, A., Ramirez, J. V., & Weber, S. (2008). The demand for football in Switzerland: An empirical estimation. *Available at SSRN 1087243*.

Bayle, E. (1999) *Management et performance des organisations à but non lucratif: le cas des fédérations sportives nationales*. Diss. Limoges.

———., & Madella, A. (2002). Development of a taxonomy of performance for national sport organizations. *European Journal of Sport Science, 2*(2), 1–21.

———., & Robinson, L. (2007). A framework for understanding the performance of national governing bodies of sport. *European Sport Management Quarterly, 7*(3), 249–268.

Belhadj, B. (2012). New weighting scheme for the dimensions in multidimensional poverty indices. *Economics Letters*, *116*(3), 304–307.

Benítez, J., Izquierdo, J., Pérez-García, R., & Ramos-Martínez, E. (2014). A simple formula to find the closest consistent matrix to a reciprocal matrix. *Applied Mathematical Modelling*, *38*(15), 3968–3974.

Benjamin, D. J., Heffetz, O., Kimball, M. S., & Szembrot, N. (2014). Beyond happiness and satisfaction: Toward well-being indices based on stated preference. *The American Economic Review*, *104*(9), 2698–2735.

Bloom, M., Hughes, D., & Gagnon, N. (2006). *Achieving Excellence: Valuing Canada's Participation in High Performance Sport: Report*. Conference Board of Canada.

Bocketti, G. P. (2008). Italian immigrants, Brazilian football, and the dilemma of national identity. *Journal of Latin American Studies*, *40*(2), 275–302.

Boeri, T., & Severgnini, B. (2014). The decline of professional football in Italy. In Goddard J., Sloane P. (eds.). *Handbook on the Economics of Professional Football*, 1–22. Cheltenham: Edward Elgar Publishing.

Böhringer, C., & Jochem, P. E. (2007). Measuring the immeasurable—A survey of sustainability indices. *Ecological Economics*, *63*(1), 1–8.

Boltvinik, J. (1998). Poverty measurement methods: An overview. SEPED Series on Poverty Reduction, UNDP, New York. Retrieved February 22, 2017, from http://www.undp.org/poverty/publications/pov_red/Poverty_Measurement_Methods.pdf

Bonsón, E., & Ratkai, M. (2013). A set of metrics to assess stakeholder engagement and social legitimacy on a corporate Facebook page. *Online Information Review*, *37*(5), 787–803.

Booysen, F. (2002). An overview and evaluation of composite indices of development. *Social Indicators Research*, *59*(2), 115–151.

Boudreaux, C. J., Boudreaux, C. J., Karahan, G., Karahan, G., Coats, M., & Coats, M. (2016). Bend it like FIFA: Corruption on and off the pitch. *Managerial Finance*, *42*(9), 866–878.

Brandolini, A. (2008). On applying synthetic indices of multidimensional well-being: Health and income inequalities in selected EU countries. *Bank of Italy Temi di Discussione (Working Paper) No*, *668*.

Bravo, G. (2014). The Human Sustainable Development Index: New calculations and a first critical analysis. *Ecological Indicators*, *37*, 145–150.

Brown, W. A. (2002). Inclusive governance practices in nonprofit organizations and implications for practice. *Nonprofit Management and Leadership*, *12*(4), 369–385.

Bryson, J. M. (2004). What to do when stakeholders matter: Stakeholder identification and analysis techniques. *Public Management Review*, *6*(1), 21–53.

Buraimo, B. (2008). Stadium attendance and television audience demand in English league football. *Managerial and Decision Economics*, *29*(6), 513–523.

Buraimo, B., & Simmons, R. (2009). Market size and attendance in English Premier League football. *International Journal of Sport Management and Marketing*, *6*(2), 200–214.

———. (2015). Uncertainty of outcome or star quality? Television audience demand for English Premier League football. *International Journal of the Economics of Business*, *22*(3), 449–469.

Chadwick, S. (2009). From outside lane to inside track: Sport management research in the twenty-first century. *Management Decision*, *47*(1), 191–203.

Chatterjee, S. K. (2005). Measurement of human development: An alternative approach. *Journal of Human Development*, *6*(1), 31–44.

Chelladurai, P., Szyszlo, M., & Haggerty, T. R. (1987). Systems-based dimensions of effectiveness-the case of national sport organizations. *Canadian Journal of Sport Sciences-revue Canadienne des sciences du sport*, *12*(2), 111–119.

Chowdhury, S., & Squire, L. (2006). Setting weights for aggregate indices: An application to the commitment to development index and human development index. *Journal of Development Studies*, *42*(5), 761–771.

Coalter, F. (2010). The politics of sport-for-development: Limited focus programmes and broad gauge problems? *International Review for the Sociology of Sport*, *45*(3), 295–314.

———., (2004). Stuck in the blocks? A sustainable sporting legacy. In A. Vigor, M. Mean and C. Tims, eds. *After the Gold Rush: A Sustainable Olympics for London*. London: Institute for Public

Collins, M. (1995). *Sports development locally and regionally*. Reading: Institute of Leisure & Amenity Management.

Crampton, J. (2004). GIS and geographic governance: Reconstructing the choropleth map. *Cartographica: The International Journal for Geographic Information and Geovisualization*, *39*(1), 41–53.

Cronbach, L. J. (1951). Coefficient alpha and the internal structure of tests. *Psychometrika*, *16*(3), 297–334.

Cushion, C. J. (2010). Coach behaviour. *Sports Coaching Professionalization and Practice*, 243–253.

Darren J, B., & Geraldine A, N. (2010). Talent development in adolescent team sports: A review. *International Journal of Sports Physiology and Performance*, *5*(1), 103–116.

De Bosscher, V., De Knop, P., Van Bottenburg, M., & Shibli, S. (2006). A conceptual framework for analysing sports policy factors leading to international sporting success. *European Sport Management Quarterly*, *6*(2), 185–215.

———., & Bingham, J. (2009). Explaining international sporting success: An international comparison of elite sport systems and policies in six countries. *Sport Management Review*, *12*(3), 113–136.

Decancq, K., & Lugo, M. A. (2013). Weights in multidimensional indices of wellbeing: An overview. *Econometric Reviews*, *32*(1), 7–34.

Dejonghe, T. (2006). The evolution of Belgian football over the last decades. Nyon, May 2, UEFA, 1–16.

———., & Van Opstal, W. (2010). Competitive balance between national leagues in European football after the Bosman case. *Rivista di Diritto ed Economia dello Sport*, *6*(2), 41–61.

Deloitte. (2014). All to play for. *Football Money League*.

———. (2015). Commercial breaks. *Football Money League*.
———. (2016). Top of the table. *Football Money League*.
———. (2017). Planet football. *Football Money League*.
European-football-statistics.co.uk. (2015). *EFS attendances*. [online] Retrieved March 14, 2016, from http://www.european-football-statistics.co.uk/attn.htm.
Ferkins, L., & Shilbury, D. (2015). The stakeholder dilemma in sport governance: Toward the notion of "stakeowner". *Journal of Sport Management, 29*(1), 93–108.
———., McDonald, G., & Shilbury, D. (2010). A model for improving board performance: The case of a national sport organisation. *Journal of Management & Organization, 16*, 633–653
———., Shilbury, D., & McDonald, G. (2005). The role of the board in building strategic capability: Towards an integrated model of sport governance research. *Sport Management Review, 8*(3), 195–225.
FIBA. (2017). *Kosovo becomes 215th National Member Federation of FIBA*. [online]. Retrieved July 24, 2017, from http://www.fiba.com/news/kosovo-becomes-215th-national-member-federation-of-fiba.
FIDE. (2017). *World chess federation*. [online] Ratings.fide.com. Retrieved July 24, 2017, from https://ratings.fide.com/fide_directory.phtml.
FIFA. (2016a). FIFA forward football development programme. Retrieved February 22, 2017, from http://www.fifa.com/development/fifa-forward-programme/index.html
———. (2016b). FIFA statutes. Retrieved February 22, 2017, from http://www.fifa.com/about-fifa/who-we-are/the-statutes.html
———. (2017). *FIFA associations and confederations—FIFA.com*. [online]. Retrieved July 24, 2017, from http://www.fifa.com/associations/index.html.
FINA. (2017). *National federations*. [online] Fina.org. Retrieved July 24, 2017, http://www.fina.org/national-federations.
FIVB. (2017). *Structure and organisation*. [online] Fivb.org. Retrieved July 24, 2017, http://www.fivb.org/EN/FIVB/FIVB_Structure.asp.
Fischer, E., & Reuber, A. R. (2011). Social interaction via new social media: (How) can interactions on Twitter affect effectual thinking and behavior?. *Journal of Business Venturing, 26*(1), 1–18.
Fleurbaey, M. (2008). *Individual well-being and social welfare: Notes on the theory*. Commission on the Measurement of Economic Performance and Social Progress.
———., & Blanchet, D. (2013). *Beyond GDP: Measuring welfare and assessing sustainability*. Oxford: Oxford University Press.
Foa, R., & Tanner, J. (2012). Methodology of the indices of social development (No. 2012–04). for maps. *The Cartographic Journal, 40*(1): 27–37.
Forster, J. (2006). Global sports organisations and their governance. *Corporate Governance: The International Journal of Business in Society, 6*(1), 72–83.
Foster, J. E., McGillivray, M., & Seth, S. (2013). Composite indices: Rank robustness, statistical association, and redundancy. *Econometric Reviews, 32*(1), 35–56.
Freeman, R. Edward. (1984). *Strategic management: A stakeholder approach*. Boston: Pitman Publishing Inc.

Freudenberg, M. (2003). Composite indicators of country performance: A critical assessment. *OECD Science, Technology and Industry Working Papers*, 2003/16, OECD Publishing, Paris.

Frick, B., & Wicker, P. (2015). The trickle-down effect: how elite sporting success affects amateur participation in German football. *Applied Economics Letters*, *23*(4), 1–5.

Frisby, W. (1986). Measuring the organizational effectiveness of national sport governing bodies. *Canadian Journal of Applied Sport Sciences*, *11*(2), 94–99.

Fukuda-Parr, S. (2001). Indicators of human development and human rights—Overlaps, differences . . . and what about the human development index? *Statistical Journal of the United Nations Economic Commission for Europe*, *18*(2, 3), 239–248.

Gaertner, W., & Xu, Y. (2006). Capability sets as the basis of a new measure of human development. *Journal of Human Development*, *7*(3), 311–321.

Gallagher, D., O'Connor, C., & Gilmore, A. (2016). An exploratory examination of the strategic direction of the Gaelic Athletic Association via the application of sports marketing segmentation bases. *Marketing Intelligence & Planning*, *34*(2), 203–222.

Gammelsæter, H., & Senaux, B. (2013). The governance of the game: A review of the research on football's governance. In Söderman S., Dolles H. (eds.) *Handbook of Research on Sport and Business*, 142–160. Cheltenham: Edward Elgar Publishing.

Gásquez, R., & Royuela, V. (2014). Is football an indicator of development at the international level? *Social Indicators Research*, *117*(3), 827–848.

Gerlitz, C., & Helmond, A. (2013). The like economy: Social buttons and the data-intensive web. *New Media & Society*, 1461444812472322.

Global Football Ranks. (2017). *CAF club ranking*. [online] Globalfootballranks.com. Retrieved July 24, 2017, http://globalfootballranks.com/en/Africa-Teams-Ranking.

Green, M. (2006). From "sport for all" to not about "sport" at all?: Interrogating sport policy interventions in the United Kingdom. *European Sport Management Quarterly*, *6*(3), 217–238.

———. (2007). Olympic glory or grassroots development?: Sport policy priorities in Australia, Canada and the United Kingdom, 1960–2006. *The International Journal of the History of Sport*, *24*(7), 921–953.

———., & Houlihan, B. (2005). *Elite sport development: Policy learning and political priorities*. Abingdon: Psychology Press.

Greyling, T., & Tregenna, F. (2014). Construction and analysis of a composite quality of life index for a region of South Africa. *Social Indicators Research*, *131*(3), 1–44.

Grix, J., & Carmichael, F. (2012). Why do governments invest in elite sport? A Polemic. *International Journal of Sport Policy and Politics*, *4*(1), 73–90.

Gürtler, O., Lang, M., & Pawlowski, T. (2015). On the release of players to national teams. *Journal of Sports Economics*, *16*(7), 695–713.

Hallmann, K., Wicker, P., Breuer, C., & Schönherr, L. (2012). Understanding the importance of sport infrastructure for participation in different sports–findings from multi-level modeling. *European Sport Management Quarterly*, *12*(5), 525–544.

Hamel, G. (2009). Moon shots for management. *Harvard Business Review*, *87*(2), 91–98.

Hanstad, D & Skille, E (2010). Does elite sport develop mass sport? *Proceedings of the Scandinavian Sport Studies Forum*, Vol. 1, 51–68

Harbison, F. H., & Myers, C. A. (1964). *Education, manpower, and economic growth: Strategies of human resource development*. Columbus: Tata McGraw-Hill Education.

Harrison, T. M., & Sayogo, D. S. (2014). Transparency, participation, and accountability practices in open government: A comparative study. *Government Information Quarterly*, *31*(4), 513–525.

Harrower, M., & Brewer, C. A. (2003). ColorBrewer. org: An online tool for selecting colour schemes for maps. *The Cartographic Journal*, *40*(1), 27–37.

Henry, I., & Lee, P. C. (2004). Governance and ethics in sport. In Beech J., Chadwick S. (eds.) *The Business of Sport Management*, 25–41. London: Pearson Education.

Hicks, N., & Streeten, P. (1979). Indicators of development: The search for a basic needs yardstick. *World Development*, *7*(6), 567–580.

Hoffmann, R., Ging, L. C., & Ramasamy, B. (2002). The socio-economic determinants of international soccer performance. *Journal of Applied Economics*, *5*(2), 253–272.

Holt, M. (2006). UEFA, governance and the control of club competition in European football. *Football Governance Research Centre, Birkbeck University*.

Hongli & Junchen. (2010). The Credit Rating of Small and Medium-sized Enterprises Based on the Grey Hierarchy Evaluation Model. *The 2nd International Conference on Information Science and Engineering: 3247–3250*. DOI: 10.1109/ICISE.2010.5689927

Houlihan, B., & Green, M. (Eds.). (2010). *Routledge handbook of sports development*. London: Routledge.

Houston, R. G., & Wilson, D. P. (2002). Income, leisure and proficiency: An economic study of football performance. *Applied Economics Letters*, *9*(14), 939–943.

Hylton, K. (Ed.). (2013). *Sports development*. London: Routledge.

———. & Bramham, P. (Eds.). (2008). *Sports development: Policy, process and practice*. London: Routledge.

IAAF (2017). *Member federations*. [online] iaaf.org. Retrieved July 24, 2017, https://www.iaaf.org/about-iaaf/structure/member-federations.

Iacus, S. M., Porro, G., Salini, S., & Siletti, E. (2015). Social networks, happiness and health: From sentiment analysis to a multidimensional indicator of subjective well-being. *arXiv preprint arXiv:1512.01569*.

IHF. (2017). *Member federations*. [online] Ihf.info. Retrieved July 24, 2017, http://www.ihf.info/en-us/theihf/memberfederations.aspx.

ITF. (2017). *Tennis history*. [online] Itftennis.com. Retrieved July 24, 2017, http://www.itftennis.com/about/organisation/history.aspx.

ITTF. (2017). *Directory—Members*. [online] International Table Tennis Federation. Retrieved July 24, 2017, http://www.ittf.com/directory/.

Ivaldi, E., Bonatti, G., & Soliani, R. (2016). The construction of a synthetic index comparing multidimensional well-being in the European Union. *Social Indicators Research*, *125*(2), 397–430.

Kaissidis-Rodafinos, A., & Anshel, M. H. (2000). Psychological predictors of coping responses among Greek basketball referees. *The Journal of Social Psychology*, *140*(3), 329–344.

Karminsky, A., & Polozov, A. (2016). A universal solution to the problem of ratings and rankings in sports. In *Handbook of Ratings* (pp. 201–226). Cham: Springer International Publishing.

Kleven, H. J., Landais, C., & Saez, E. (2013). Taxation and international migration of superstars: Evidence from the European football market. *The American Economic Review*, *103*(5), 1892–1924.

Klugman, J., Rodríguez, F., & Choi, H. J. (2011). The HDI 2010: New controversies, old critiques. *Journal of Economic Inequality*, *9*(2), 249–288.

Kohonen, T. (1982). Self-organized formation of topologically correct feature maps. *Biological Cybernetics*, *43*(1), 59–69.

Kovacevic, M. (2010). Review of HDI critiques and potential improvements. *Human Development Research Paper*, 33.

Krishnakumar, J., & Nagar, A. L. (2008). On exact statistical properties of multidimensional indices based on principal components, factor analysis, MIMIC and structural equation models. *Social Indicators Research*, *86*(3), 481–496.

Kruse SE. (2006) Review of kicking AIDS out: Is sport an effective tool in the fight against HIV/AIDS? Draft report to NORAD, unpublished.

Kuper, S., & Szymanski, S. (2010). *Why England lose: & other curious football phenomena explained*. London: HarperCollins UK.

Labib, A. W., Williams, G. B., & O'Connor, R. F. (1998). An intelligent maintenance model (system): An application of the analytic hierarchy process and a fuzzy logic rule-based controller. *Journal of the Operational Research Society*, *49*(7), 745–757.

Larcker, D. F., Richardson, S. A., & Tuna, I. (2007). Corporate governance, accounting outcomes, and organizational performance. *The Accounting Review*, *82*(4), 963–1008.

Lasek, J., Szlávik, Z., & Bhulai, S. (2013). The predictive power of ranking systems in association football. *International Journal of Applied Pattern Recognition*, *1*(1), 27–46.

———., Gagolewski, M., & Bhulai, S. (2016). How to improve a team's position in the FIFA ranking? A simulation study. *Journal of Applied Statistics*, *43*(7), 1349–1368.

Leeds, M. A., & Marikova Leeds, E. (2009). International soccer success and national institutions. *Journal of Sports Economics*, *10*(4), 369–390.

Lehtonen, M. (2015). Indicators: Tools for informing, monitoring or controlling. In *The Tools of Policy Formulation: Actors, Capacities, Venues and Effects* (pp. 76–99). Cheltenham: Edward Elgar.

Levermore, R. (2009). Sport-in-international development: Theoretical frameworks. In *Sport and International Development* (pp. 26–54). Basingstoke: Palgrave Macmillan UK.

Lim, S. Y., Warner, S., Dixon, M., Berg, B., Kim, C., & Newhouse-Bailey, M. (2011). Sport participation across national contexts: A multilevel investigation of individual and systemic influences on adult sport participation. *European Sport Management Quarterly, 11*(3), 197–224.

Limstrand, T., & Rehrer, N. J. (2008). Young people's use of sports facilities: A Norwegian study on physical activity. *Scandinavian Journal of Social Medicine, 36*(5), 452–459.

Loewenthal, K. M. (1996). *An introduction to psychological tests and scales*. London: UCL Press.

Lorenz, J., Brauer, C., & Lorenz, D. (2016). Rank-Optimal Weighting or "How to be Best in the OECD Better Life Index?" *Social Indicators Research*, 1–18.

MacMahon, C., Helsen, W. F., Starkes, J. L., & Weston, M. (2007). Decision-making skills and deliberate practice in elite association football referees. *Journal of Sports Sciences, 25*(1), 65–78.

MacNeil, S., & Elmqvist, N. (2013, September). Visualization mosaics for multivariate visual exploration. *Computer Graphics Forum, 32*(6), 38–50.

Madella, A., Bayle E., & J. Tome. (2005). The organisational performance of national swimming federations in Mediterranean countries: A comparative approach. *European Journal of Sport Science, 5*(4), 207–220.

Maderer, D., Holtbrügge, D., & Schuster, T. (2014). Professional football squads as multicultural teams: Cultural diversity, intercultural experience, and team performance. *International Journal of Cross Cultural Management, 14*(2), 215–238.

Mangan, S., & Collins, K. (2016). A rating system for Gaelic Football Teams: Factors that influence success. *International Journal of Computer Science in Sport, 15*(2), 78–90.

Manuel Luiz, J., & Fadal, R. (2011). An economic analysis of sports performance in Africa. *International Journal of Social Economics, 38*(10), 869–883.

Martindale, R. J., Collins, D., & Abraham, A. (2007). Effective talent development: The elite coach perspective in UK sport. *Journal of Applied Sport Psychology, 19*(2), 187–206.

Mascarenhas, D. R., Collins, D., & Mortimer, P. (2005). Elite refereeing performance: Developing a model for sport science support. *Sport Psychologist, 19*, 364–379.

McGillivray, M., & Noorbakhsh, F. (2007). Composite indexes of human well-being: Past, present and future. In *Human Well-Being* (pp. 113–134). Basingstoke: Palgrave Macmillan UK.

McGranahan, D. (1972). Development indicators and development models. *The Journal of Development Studies, 8*(3), 91–102.

Merriam-Webster Dictionary. (2017). Retrieved March 3, 2017, from https://www.merriam-webster.com/dictionary/popular

Michie, J., & Oughton, C. (2004). *Competitive balance in football: Trends and effects*. London: The sportsnexus.

Miragaia, D. A. M., Ferreira, J., & Carreira, A. (2014). Do stakeholders matter in strategic decision making of a sports organization? *Revista de Administração de Empresas, 54*(6), 647–658.

Miranda, F. J., Chamorro, A., Rubio, S., & Rodriguez, O. (2014). Professional sports teams on social networks: A comparative study employing the Facebook assessment index. *International Journal of Sport Communication, 7*(1), 74–89.

Morris, M. D. (1978). A physical quality of life index. *Urban Ecology*, *3*(3), 225–240.

Moura, F. A., Martins, L. E. B., & Cunha, S. A. (2014). Analysis of football game-related statistics using multivariate techniques. *Journal of Sports Sciences*, *32*(20), 1881–1887.

Munda, G., & Nardo, M. (2005). Constructing consistent composite indicators: The issue of weights. *EUR 21834 EN*.

Nardo, M., Saisana, M., Saltelli, A., Tarantola, S., Hoffman, A., & Giovannini, E. (2008). *Handbook on constructing composite indices: Methodology and user guide*. Paris: OECD Publishing, 162 pp.

Nauright, J. (2004). Global games: Culture, political economy and sport in the globalised world of the 21st century. *Third World Quarterly*, *25*(7), 1325–1336.

Neale, W. C. (1964). The peculiar economics of professional sports. *The Quarterly Journal of Economics*, *78*(1), 1–14.

Neumayer, E. (2001). The human development index and sustainability—A constructive proposal. *Ecological Economics*, *39*(1), 101–114.

Nicoletti, G., Scarpetta, S., & Boylaud, O. (1999). Summary indicators of product market regulation with an extension to employment protection legislation. Paris: OECD, ECO Working Paper No. 226.

Njororai, W. W. S. (2017). Organizational factors influencing football development in East African countries. *Soccer & Society*, 1–21.

Noorbakhsh, F. (1998). The human development index: Some technical issues and alternative indices. *Journal of International Development*, *10*(5), 589–605.

OECD. (2015). Gross Domestic Product (GDP). Retrieved September 10, from https://stats.oecd.org/glossary/detail.asp?ID=1163 ().

Ostroff, C., & Schmitt, N. (1993). Configurations of organizational effectiveness and efficiency. *Academy of Management Journal*, *36*(6), 1345–1361.

Otley, D. (1999). Performance management: A framework for management control systems research. *Management Accounting Research*, *10*(4), 363–382.

Palazzi, P., & Lauri, A. (2013). The human development index: Suggested corrections. *PSL Quarterly Review*, *51*(205), 193–221

Pang, B., & Lee, L. (2005, June). Seeing stars: Exploiting class relationships for sentiment categorization with respect to rating scales. In *Proceedings of the 43rd Annual Meeting on Association for Computational Linguistics* (pp. 115–124). Association for Computational Linguistics.

Parent, M. M., & Séguin, B. (2007). Factors that led to the drowning of a world championship organizing committee: A stakeholder approach. *European Sport Management Quarterly*, *7*(2), 187–212.

Paruolo, P., Saisana, M., & Saltelli, A. (2013). Ratings and rankings: Voodoo or science?. *Journal of the Royal Statistical Society: Series A (Statistics in Society)*, *176*(3), 609–634.

PASTILLE Consortium (2002). *Indicators into Action: Local Sustainability Indicator Sets in their Context*. Final report.

Pate, S. K., & Sweo, R. (2016). The Social Progress Index in international business site selection: Three case studies. *Journal of International Education and Leadership Volume*, *6*(2), 1–10.

Pawlowski, T., & Anders, C. (2012). Stadium attendance in German professional football—The (un) importance of uncertainty of outcome reconsidered. *Applied Economics Letters, 19*(16), 1553–1556.

Pérez, C. C., Bolívar, M. P. R., & Hernández, A. M. L. (2012). The use of web 2.0 to transform public services delivery: The case of Spain. In *Web 2.0 Technologies and Democratic Governance* (pp. 41–61). New York: Springer.

Pinheiro-Alves, R., & Zambujal-Oliveira, J. (2012). The Ease of Doing Business Index as a tool for investment location decisions. *Economics Letters, 117*(1), 66–70.

Plumley, D., Wilson, R., & Ramchandani, G. (2017). Towards a model for measuring holistic performance of professional Football clubs. *Soccer & Society, 18*(1), 1–14.

Policy Research/Demos.London East Research Institute. (2007). *Lasting legacy for London? Assessing the legacy of the Olympic games and paralympic games*. London: University of East London, LERI.

Ranis, G., Stewart, F., & Samman, E. (2006). Human development: Beyond the human development index. *Journal of Human Development, 7*(3), 323–358.

Ravallion, M. (1997). Good and bad growth: The human development reports. *World Development, 25*(5): 631–638.

———. (2012). Troubling tradeoffs in the human development index. *Journal of Development Economics, 99*(2), 201–209.

Render, B., Stair, R. M., & Harpell, J. L. (1991). *Quantitative analysis for management: Study guide*. Boston: Allyn and Bacon.

Rohde, M., & Breuer, C. (2016). Europe's Elite Football: Financial growth, sporting success, transfer investment, and private majority investors. *International Journal of Financial Studies, 4*(2), 12.

Rösch, D., Hodgson, R., Peterson, L., Graf-Baumann, T., Junge, A., Chomiak, J., & Dvorak, J. (2000). Assessment and evaluation of football performance. *The American Journal of Sports Medicine, 28*(suppl 5), S-29.

Rowley, T. J. (1997). Moving beyond dyadic ties: A network theory of stakeholder influences. *Academy of Management Review, 22*(4), 887–910.

Rydin, Y. (2002). *Indicators into action: Local sustainability indicator sets in their context*. London, UK: The Pastille Consortium, London School of Economics.

Saaty, T. L. (1988). What is the analytic hierarchy process?. In *Mathematical Models for Decision Support* (pp. 109–121). Berlin: Springer Heidelberg.

Santeramo, F. G. (2015). On the composite indicators for food security: Decisions matter! *Food Reviews International, 31*(1), 63–73.

Santos, M. E. and G. Santos (2014). Composite indices of development. In B. Currie-Alder, R. Kanbur, D. Malone, and R. Medhora eds. *International Development: Ideas, Experience and Prospects* (pp. 133–150). Oxford: Oxford University Press.

Scelles, N. (2017). Star quality and competitive balance? Television audience demand for English Premier League football reconsidered. *Applied Economics Letters, 19*(24), 1–4.

Scelles, N., & Andreff, W. (2014). How to predict the 2014 World Cup winner (in one simple equation): Determinants of national football team results 2011-2013—A new methodology. *Fraser of Allander Institute Economic Commentary, 38*(1), 100–103.

———., Durand, C., Bonnal, L., Goyeau, D., & Andreff, W. (2016). Do all sporting prizes have a significant positive impact on attendance in a European national football league? Competitive intensity in the French Ligue 1. *Ekonomicheskaya Politika/Economic Policy, 11*(3), 82–107.

Schlesinger, W., Taulet, A. C., Alves, H., & Burguete, J. L. V. (2016). An approach to measuring perceived quality of life in the city through a formative multidimensional perspective. In *Entrepreneurial and Innovative Practices in Public Institutions* (pp. 59–79). Cham: Springer International Publishing.

Senaux, B. (2008). A stakeholder approach to football club governance. *International Journal of Sport Management and Marketing, 4*(1), 4–17.

Shilbury, D., Ferkins, L., & Smythe, L. (2013). Sport governance encounters: Insights from lived experiences. *Sport Management Review, 16*(3), 349–363.

Social Progress Imperative. (2016). 2016 Social Progress Index Methodological Report. Retrieved February 22, 2017. http://www.socialprogressimperative.org/publication/2016-social-progress-index-methodological-report/

Solberg, H. A. (2008). The international trade of players in European club football: Consequences for national teams. *International Journal of Sports Marketing and Sponsorship, 10*(1), 73–87.

Stefani, R. (2011). The methodology of officially recognized international sports rating systems. *Journal of Quantitative Analysis in Sports, 7*(4), Article 10.

Stefani, R. T. (1997). Survey of the major world sports rating systems. *Journal of Applied Statistics, 24*(6), 635–646.

Streeten, P. (1981). The distinctive features of a basic-needs approach to development. In *Development Perspectives* (pp. 334–365). London: Palgrave Macmillan UK.

———. (1994). Human development: Means and ends. *American Economic Review* (Papers and Proceedings), *84*(2): 232–237.

Szymanski, S. (2010). The market for soccer players in England after Bosman: Winners and losers. In *Football Economics and Policy* (pp. 27–51). London: Palgrave Macmillan UK.

Tacon, R. (2007). Football and social inclusion: Evaluating social policy. *Managing Leisure, 12*(1), 1–23.

Tan, T. C., Huang, H. C., Bairner, A., & Chen, Y. W. (2016). Xi Jin-Ping's World Cup dreams: From a major sports country to a world sports power. *The International Journal of the History of Sport, 33*(12), 1–17.

Teodor, D. & Adrian, O. (2015). A composite index to assess the top European Football Clubs in 2014. *Revista Economică, 67*(2), 68–85

Ter, H. G., Gammelsæter, H., & Senaux, B. (Eds.). (2011). *The organisation and governance of top football across Europe: An institutional perspective*. London: Routledge.

Tomao, A., Secondi, L., Corona, P., Giuliarelli, D., Quatrini, V., & Agrimi, M. (2015). Can composite indices explain multidimensionality of tree risk assessment? A case study in an historical monumental complex. *Urban Forestry & Urban Greening, 14*(3), 456–465.

Trame, J., & Keßler, C. (2011). Exploring the lineage of volunteered geographic information with heat maps. Hamburg: GeoViz.
UEFA. (2015). *UEFA rankings for club competitions.* Retrieved March 3, 2015, from http://www.uefa.com/memberassociations/uefarankings/country/index.html
———. (2017). *UEFA Rankings for club competitions.* Retrieved February 22, 2017. http://www.uefa.com/memberassociations/uefarankings/club/
Ülengin, B., Ülengin, F., & Güvenç, Ü. (2001). A multidimensional approach to urban quality of life: The case of Istanbul. *European Journal of Operational Research, 130*(2), 361–374.
UNDP. (2010). *Human Development Report Nigeria 2008–2009. Achieving Growth with Equity.* New York: United Nations Development Programme.
———. (2014). Methodology papers. Retrieved February 22, 2017. http://hdr.undp.org/en/paper-categories/methodology-papers
United Nations (2005) *Sport for Development and Peace: Towards Achieving the Millennium Development Goals.* New York: United Nations.
United Nations Development Programme. Human Development Report 2014. Retrieved September 10, 2015 from http://hdr.undp.org/en/content/human-development-report-2014.
Vail, S. E. (2007). Community development and sport participation. *Journal of Sport Management, 21*(4), 571–596.
Vorobyev, A., Zarova, E., Solntsev, I., Osokin, N., & Zhulevich, V. (2016). Statistical evaluation of football performance depending on the socio-economic development of countries. *Statistical Journal of the IAOS, 32*(3), 403–411.
Vrooman, J. (2007). Theory of the beautiful game: The unification of European football. *Scottish Journal of Political Economy, 54*(3), 314–354.
Wagner, D. A. (2005). *Monitoring and measuring literacy.* Paris, France: United Nations Educational, Scientific and Cultural Organization.
Walters, G., & Tacon, R. (2010). Corporate social responsibility in sport: Stakeholder management in the UK football industry. *Journal of Management & Organization, 16*(04), 566–586.
Well, D. N. (2007). Accounting for the effect of health on economic growth. *The Quarterly Journal of Economics, 122*(3), 1265–1306.
Wicker, P., & Breuer, C. (2011). Scarcity of resources in German non-profit sport clubs. *Sport Management Review, 14*(2), 188–201.
Wicker, P., Breuer, C., & Pawlowski, T. (2009). Promoting sport for all to age-specific target groups: The impact of sport infrastructure. *European Sport Management Quarterly, 9*(2), 103–118.
———. (2009). Promoting sport for all to age-specific target groups: The impact of sport infrastructure. *European Sport Management Quarterly, 9*(2), 103–118.
Winand, M., Rihoux, B., Qualizza, D., & Zintz, T. (2011). Combinations of key determinants of performance in sport governing bodies. *Sport, Business and Management: An International Journal, 1*(3), 234–251.
———., Zintz, T., Bayle, E., & Robinson, L. (2010). Organizational performance of Olympic sport governing bodies: Dealing with measurement and priorities. *Managing Leisure, 15*(4), 279–307.

Winkler, W. E. (1988). Using the EM algorithm for weight computation in the Fellegi-Sunter model of record linkage. In *Proceedings of the Section on Survey Research Methods, American Statistical Association,* Vol. 667, 671.

Wolfe, R. A., & Putler, D. S. (2002). How tight are the ties that bind stakeholder groups? *Organization Science, 13*(1), 64–80.

Wood, D. J. 1994. *Business and society* (2nd ed.). NewYork: HarperCollins.

Worldfootball.net. (2017). *worldfootball.net.* [online]. Retrieved July 24, 2017, http://www.worldfootball.net/.

World Bank. 2015 GDP per capita (current US$), Retrieved September 10, 2015, from http://data.worldbank.org/indicator/NY.GDP.PCAP.CD

Worldstadiums.com. (2017). *World stadiums.* [online]. Retrieved July 24, 2017, http://www.worldstadiums.com/.

Yusof, M. M., Sulaiman, T., Khalid, R., Hamid, M. S. A., & Mansor, R. (2014, December). Rating competitors before tournament starts: How it's affecting team progression in a soccer tournament. In H. Ibrahim, J. Zulkepli, N. Aziz, N. Ahmad, and S. A. Rahman eds. *AIP Conference Proceedings, 1635*(1), 665–670.

Zerguini, Y., Dvorak, J., Maughan, R. J., Leiper, J. B., Bartagi, Z., Kirkendall, D. T. & Junge, A. (2008). Influence of Ramadan fasting on physiological and performance variables in football players: summary of the F-MARC 2006 Ramadan fasting study. *Journal of Sports Sciences, 26*(S3), S3–S6.

Index

Note: Page references for figures are *italicized*

AFC. *See* Asian Football Confederation
Asian Football Confederation, 23, 54, *57, 107*

Bosman case, 6, 28

CAF. *See* Confederation of African Football
coaches, 49
competitive balance, 20, 31
composite indicator, 1, 10, 37
Confederation of African Football, 23–24, 54, *58, 107*

Federation of International Football Associations:
    Coca-Cola ranking, 1, 20–22, 28, 49–50, *52*, 63, 74;
    structure, 6, 23, 25, 28;
    Women's World Ranking, 22–23, 28, *52*;
    World Cup, 6, 49, 79
FIFA. *See* Federation of International Football Associations

GDP. *See* Gross domestic product
grassroots, 29–30, 47, 79

Gross domestic product, 9, 54, 64

HDI. *See* Human Development Index
Human Development Index, 11–15, 36, 40, 74

match attendance, 31, 36, 48, 61

referees, 30

Social Progress Index, 18–20, 34, 46
SPI. *See* Social Progress Index
sport governance, 2
sport participation. *See* grassroots
sports development, 3–4
sports infrastructure, 30

TV demand, 30–31

UEFA. *See* Union of European Football Associations
UNDP. *See* United Nations Development Programme
Union of European Football Associations, 6, 23, 28, *58, 109*
United Nations Development Programme, 11, 27, 65–66

121

About the Authors

Nikita Osokin is head analyst of the Center of Strategic Sport Research at Plekhanov Russian University of Economics. His main research interests include performance measurement and management within sports, strategic management in sports, North-American sports, sport policy, international sports development, competitive balance.

Ilya Solntsev is the Director of the Center of Strategic Sport Research at Plekhanov Russian University of Economics. He is one of the coauthors of "Football development strategy of Russian Federation until 2020" and member of two committees within Football Union of Russia: "Football development programs" and "Appeal committee regarding licensing of football clubs". Dr. Solntsev participated in drafting a report for the President of Russian Federation about development of football in Russia and preparation for the World Cup 2018. His main research interests include value creation in sports industry; financial valuation of sport organizations and sport facilities; consumer preferences of football fans and loyalty programs; economic impact of sport events; applying rating models for evaluation of sports organizations.

Anatoly Vorobyev is the Head of Department of Sports Management and Marketing at Plekhanov Russian University of Economics. From 1992 to 1997, he was the first vice-president and later CEO of Dinamo Moscow Football Club. He participated in forming the first development strategy for Russian football in 1994. From 2012 to 2015, he held the position of General Secretary at the Football Union of Russia. His main research interests include performance management within sports, finances of sports organizations, strategic management in sports, collegiate sports.

www.ingramcontent.com/pod-product-compliance
Ingram Content Group UK Ltd.
Pitfield, Milton Keynes, MK11 3LW, UK
UKHW040205230326
11407UKWH00001B/3

9 781498 555197